SAILING THE STRAIT

Aspects of Port Dinorwic and the Menai Strait

Reg Chambers Jones

bridge books

Wrexham

Sailing the Strait — Aspects of Port Dinorwic and the Menai Strait

first published in Wales in 2004

by

BRIDGE BOOKS
61 Park Avenue
Wrexham
LL12 7AW

© Text Reg Chambers Jones

© Design, typesetting and layout, Bridge Books, Wrexham

ISBN   1-84494-012-8

A CIP entry for this book is available from the British Library

Printed and bound by
CROMWELL PRESS
Trowbridge
Wiltshire

In memory of my beloved wife

Maureen

By the same author

Bridges and Ferries

Arian — the story of money and banking in Wales

Felinheli — a personal history of the Port of Dinorwic

Bless 'Em All — aspects of the war in north-west Wales, 1939–45

Curiouser and Curiouser — oddities in north-west Wales

Contents

Abbreviations

UCNW	University College of North Wales, Bangor
PYA	Porth yr Aur Papers (UCNW)
BP	Bangor Papers (UCNW)
LP	Lligwy Papers (UCNW)
PN	Plas Newydd Papers (UCNW)
GAS	Gwynedd Archives Service
VP	Vaynol Papers
CQS	Caernarvonshire Quarter Sessions
DQ	Dinorwic Quarry
FRO	Flintshire Record Office

Preface

It is many years since slates were being produced at Llanberis and delivered to Felinheli or to Port Dinorwic as it was then called. In the little space now left on the quayside at Felinheli which is not occupied by houses, there is now an air of tranquillity compared to the bustle, the noise and the movement caused by men, engines, wagons and ships. The dry dock whistle, that called the men to work at 7.30am, dismissed them at midday, recalled them at 1pm and dismissed them again at 5pm, has been replaced by the hooters of the yachts and cruisers, demanding to either be released from their moorings and let out of the dock, or be allowed to return to regain their sheltered positions within the one hundred year old dock where, once, a dozen or more ships would be tied up for loading with slate, or unloaded of coal or ballast.

Apart from readily available information obtainable in libraries and archives, other details which I have included in this book have been derived from private papers and personal recollections, details which were in danger of being lost to the future. It is certainly not intended to be definitive.

I should like to record my appreciation of the assistance and guidance that I have consistently received from W. Alister Williams; Dr David Gwyn, Pen-y-Groes; the staff at the Gwynedd Archives; Caernarfon Library; Library and Manuscript Department of the University of Wales, Bangor; Einion Wyn Thomas (Archivist) and staff of the Archives Department of the University of Wales, Bangor; Merseyside Maritime Museum, Albert Dock, Liverpool and the National Library of Wales, Aberystwyth.

My thanks also to the following, for allowing me access to photographs and private papers and for permission to publish them: Vernon Bowles, Alun L. Jones, Katie Withersby-Lench, Derek Paine, Emyr Wyn Roberts, Glyn and Elspeth Pritchard, Margaret Tuzuner, Charles Waine and Len Williams.

I am also grateful to the following who allowed me to make copies of private photographs, some of which have been used in the book and duly acknowledged: Andrew Dickie, Yvonne Edwards, Jean Elias, David Fowler, David Gallichan; John Hughes, William Hughes, Betty Pierce Jones, Dilys Jones, Gareth Jones, Harry Wyn Jones, Katie Limerick Jones, Roma Lort Jones, Betty Owen, Eric Owen, Geraint Owen, Joe Heber Owen, John Bryan Owen, Captain J. Rodney Parry, Ken Phillips, Della Pierce, Nancy Pierce, Vernon Pierce, Kathleen Wyn Roberts, Yvonne Roberts, Faunne Statham, Ellen Stenning, Bessie Thompson, Nancy Tildsley and Steve Williams.

Reg Chambers Jones
2004

Introduction

Slate had been quarried in the Llanberis area, on a relatively limited basis, to meet local needs until Thomas Assheton Smith (1752–1828) of Vaynol, realised the commercial value of an area which had been dismissed in the past as a mountain fit only for grazing sheep.

In 1788, he granted a lease of 21 years to three individuals who traded as the Dinorwic Slate Company. When it expired in 1809, Assheton Smith offered William Turner (1766–1853, the father of Sir Llewelyn Turner of Parkia) a partnership in the quarry, which he accepted. As an initial step, in an effort to improve the primitive working methods within the quarry, Turner introduced the system of inclines as a means of easing the task of transporting slate down the mountainside, a system which he had no doubt seen employed in the eight other slate quarries and one copper mine at Drws y Coed that he had been involved with.*

This partnership continued until 1820 when Assheton Smith, by then no doubt realising the future potential of the industry, took full control of the quarry by buying Turner's share. When Assheton Smith's son, also called Thomas (1776–1858), inherited the estate in 1828, there was an increased demand for houses and factories which required a durable and reliable roofing material: slate was found to be ideal.

Meeting the demand for slate was problematic, as the means of transporting it from the quarry to the coast presented difficulties. Once quarried, the slate was brought by boat to Penllyn at the Caernarfon end of Llyn Padarn, where it was loaded into panniers on the back of mules or ponies which were then led across country, through Llanddeiniolen to Moel y Don [PYA 29089], where the slates were lightered to waiting ships anchored on the Menai Strait [*North Wales Gazette* 20.3.1817]. In an attempt to ease this problem, Assheton Smith had built a private road in 1812 from Fachwen down Nant y Garth to Felinheli. This horse and cart method of transport continued in use until the iron tramway (*ffordd haearn*) was built in 1824, more or less following the same route.

Until the latter part of the eighteenth century, Felinheli consisted mainly of the two hamlets of Aberpwll and Tanymaes, a mile or so apart. A number of references to Aberpwll are made in the Caernarvonshire Quarter Sessions records which confirm the existence of an established community in the sixteenth century:

pp48 The Memories of Sir Llewelyn Turner.

Thomas Assheton Smith I (1752–1828) [Author]

Vaynol Hall, viewed from the south-east. [John Hughes]

'... April 15 1551, Lewis ap William Dio lately of Aberpwll, miller ...17 June 1555, Richard ap Robert ap Grono of Aber y Pull, Yeoman ... October 1557, Moris ap William ap Thomas of Aberypwll tailor ...' [CQS]

The original water-mill at Aberpwll, which had became disused due to the silting up of the nearby Afon Heilyn, was replaced by a new salt water-mill c.1633 near the seashore, on the Bangor side of the estuary, which gave the village the name of Felinheli (salt water-mill). It was worked by the ebb and flow of the tide and continued in use until 1797 (the 1778 survey of Vaynol properties compiled for Thomas Assheton Smith described it as 'mill greatly out of repair' [VP 4057]), by which time the wharfs that were being built within the mud estuary allowed a more efficient method of loading and unloading ships, when compared with the previous time-consuming method of lightering from the Moel y Don jetty. Land which had been reclaimed from the sea provided additional space for the storage of slate and new wharfs for larger vessels.

As the result of an increased quantity of slate passing through the Aberpwll area, in part caused by the new 1812 road and, subsequently, the iron railway, additional cottages for workers associated with the trade began to be built, to form the eventual small community of Siloh, adjacent to the much older hamlet of Aberpwll. During the first thirty years of the nineteenth century, three chapels were built to cater for the spiritual needs of the increasing population of the area. In addition, the children had the unusual benefit of a private school with an erudite schoolmaster; Thomas Griffiths (1781–1861) gave lessons on a range of subjects at a cost of 1d. a week per child, at a time when education was usually limited to Sunday schools.

The long established farms of Bodandreg [CQS 20 May 1552], Carreg Gwalch, Pantyrafallen and Penrallt, together with properties located at Aberpwll, twenty-seven in all, were owned by Thomas Assheton Smith c.1800. However, the land within the eventual village of Port Dinorwic and forming part of the parish of Llanfairisgaer was owned by Lord Boston, even though his main estate was in Anglesey. This precluded Assheton Smith from developing much needed land in the vicinity of the waterfront and in the village itself for some years to come.

The 1824, iron railway was replaced in 1848 by the Padarn railway. For the first five years the wagons were horse-drawn before steam engines were introduced as a means of expediting the transport of slate from the quarry to Port Dinorwic. Also, within the next four years, two other major events took place which were to change the character of the village: the completion of the mainline railway between Bangor and Caernarfon in 1852, and the replacing of the original inadequate station (built adjacent to the Halfway Inn) with a new one which not only provided easier access for passengers, but also additional space for sidings where goods and animal traffic could be handled. The London & North Western Railway, which took over the smaller railway companies, built a branch line from Port Siding to the quay which allowed slate to be loaded directly on to railway wagons.

Such dramatic changes within a relatively short space of time demanded, amongst other things, an increased workforce and the need for housing and shops for the men and their families. This was the catalyst that caused a surge of building work in Port Dinorwic from 1853, resulting in a dramatic change in the environment.

As the result of land being leased, usually, for 90 years from Lord Boston, houses and shops began to be built along Bangor Road, as it was then called, usually in multiples of two or more to form eventually either small terraces or a complete row. The variations in the style of building can be identified today. These are a few examples of such leases:

> Lease 90 years 24 June 1871 — Lord Boston to John Edwards, barometer maker, Snowdon Street, Port Dinorwic to build 2 houses at Beach Road
>
> Lease 60 years 12 November 1873 — Lord Boston to Henry Hughes, butcher to build a slaughter house on land near the beach
>
> Lease 90 years 12 November 1875 — Lord Boston to William Jones. Bangor Road, Port Dinorwic, joiner on 'land occupied by old Bush out-buildings, 10 good houses to be built' (it was on part of this land that the Arvonia shop was built)
>
> Lease 90 years 12 May 1876 — Lord Boston to Rev. Robert Jones and Capt. Griffith Williams, Frondeg Terrace, Port Dinorwic, land in Bangor Road to build Wesleyan Chapel.
>
> Lease 90 years 29 September 1880 — Lord Boston to Hugh Evans, junior, Snowdon Street, Port Dinorwic, carpenter, land in Bangor Road (an added note stated: 'which completes the land in Bangor Road up to William Jones' land' see above).

Bodlondeb Terrace, Bangor Road, consisting of three houses, was built by three brothers, including Thomas Martin Williams, in anticipation of them retiring from the sea.

According to Edmund Hyde Hall [*A Description of Caernarvonshire ...*], there were 45 dwellings housing 225 persons in and near Felinheli in 1803 but, during the period between 1841 and 1881, undoubtedly the most industrious time for the village and its inhabitants, 519 houses were built and the population of Felinheli increased from 549 to 2,020.

The turnpike road of 1776 between Bangor ferry and Caernarfon, passed through the middle of Felinheli and, in particular, through Bush farm. When it became obvious that the farm house and outbuildings would impede further development in the village and improvements to the road, it was relocated *c.*1869 on a higher part of the farmland [Bangor Papers 1162] and thereafter the new farmhouse and outbuildings were known as *Bush Newydd*. The old Bush farmhouse was listed as being unoccupied in 1873 and demolished shortly after [Bangor Papers 1167]. The outbuildings, however, were still in existence two years later (lease dated 12 November 1875 mentioned previously). It was on this site that the eventual Arvonia and Dinorwic House shops were built. Although the mainline railway had arrived at Port Dinorwic in 1852, with the line dividing Bush farmland into two, farming activities continued on this, the lower section, which extended down to the seashore, for a further 17 years.

In an area where all the farms in the periphery of Felinheli bear Welsh names, Bush Farm appears to be quite incongruous. However, on Lewis Morris's Chart of 1737–38, a time when the area was sparsely populated, one property is shown bearing the name 'Holly Bush'. The term 'Hollin Bush' or 'Holly Bush' were familiar in many parts of the country and especially so in the Lake District and south Wales where, in the days before distinctive tavern signs indicated the availability of accommodation, a branch of holly would be hung outside as an indication to drivers of pack-ponies or drovers with cattle or sheep, that land was available where animals could be held in secure compounds to water, feed and rest overnight. The fact that legal documents, dated 1861, refer to 'Bush Tavern', clearly indicates that, in addition to its normal farm activities, it was undoubtedly a tavern at one time.

The Halfway Inn, conveniently located halfway between Bangor and Caernarfon, held a licence for a billiard table and to brew its own beer in the early part of the nineteenth century. In addition to its role as a hostelry, an extension built in the latter part of the nineteenth century was used as a 'Drapery, Grocery and Chandlery Establishment' run by a Mrs Margaret Jones. The licensee also acted as postmaster at the time when a letter or postcard, bearing a halfpenny stamp, posted in a morning would be delivered locally in the afternoon of that same day.

Halfway Inn, Y Felinheli. [Yvonne Roberts]

As with the Halfway, the date when the Garddfon Inn was established is equally a matter of conjecture. However, it has been related that John Wesley stayed there in 1747 and in subsequent years whilst travelling in the area. Suitably sited near the Moel y Don ferry, no doubt it would be a welcome haven for Wesley, as it was for many others whose passage across the Strait was delayed because of adverse weather or, equally, a pleasant port of call after a rough passage across from Anglesey.

As the result of an award dated 29 August 1889 between Lord Boston and G. W. D. Assheton Smith, it was agreed that the former would sell to the latter all his property in Llanfairisgaer, including Bush Newydd, for the sum of £15,330 [Lligwy Papers 1083; Bangor Papers 1191].

By 1873, new street names had begun to appear in the village e.g. Augusta Place replacing Augusta Street. The biggest change in this respect, occurred when the general term of Garddfon, for the district adjacent to the tavern, was replaced by individual street names such as Menai Street (originally called New Street), Snowdon Street (the name first appeared in March 1861) and Beach Row which was later changed to Beach Road.

There was virtually nothing that could not be bought in the village from some thirty plus shops, whether it be for the home, farm or boat. The variety of shops included a delicatessen, wallpaper and paint shop, cake shop, a shop selling nothing else but toys, newsagents/book shops, five public houses, fishmongers, ships' chandlery, sail-makers, smithy, printer, dressmaker, shoe shops and repairers together with coal merchants, milk retailers and a tinsmith. The versatile village watchmaker also sold and repaired bicycles. The village bakeries would not only have a wide selection of confectioneries for sale, but could also bake to order home produced dough (identified with a numbered tag). There was a choice of three tailors and two hairdressers (one of whom was also a taxidermist). For those who could not afford the cost of a prescribed medicine, there was an alternative in the form of 'special medicines guaranteed to cure anything' sold at the Beehive on Snowdon Street. These 'cures' were made up, on the spot, in accordance with the symptoms described by the 'patient' and could contain a mixture of quinine, tincture of rhubarb, Indian brandy and a few other things thrown in for good measure.

In addition to these shops, whose range and quality of goods on offer were on a par, if not superior, to those available in nearby towns, it was not unusual for houses to make use of one of their rooms to either create or supplement their income, by selling firewood, candles, paraffin, fish caught in the Strait, or home-grown vegetables. Even in the 1920s, by which time electricity, generated at the dry-dock workshop, gradually came to be used in the village, a large number of households continued to use paraffin for both lighting and cooking. By the end of the First World War, many of these 'quasi -shops' had closed and, with the introduction of a local bus service, there was a tendency for villagers to take the opportunity of shopping in Bangor or Caernarfon once or twice a week, as well as in the village.

Supplies for the local shops either came by Morris & Jones steam-tractors, or by the company's coastal ship (*Christiana*) which brought supplies from Liverpool and left a variety of goods in a quay warehouse ready for re-stocking as and when required.

Since refrigeration in both homes and shops was still a thing of the future and 'sell-by' dates did not exist, shopping for food was a daily event. Saturday was a particularly busy day with most of the shops staying open until 10pm. Sundays, however, would be a 'day of rest' for everyone — apart from the newspaper shop and the milkman, delivering as usual by horse and cart. The local abattoir, located in a small stone-built building at the bottom of Snowdon Street, where local butchers did their own slaughtering by pole-axing animals, would ensure that the meat was fresh.

William Owen's boot and shoe repair shop, lit by a single paraffin lamp hung from the ceiling, was the place where the village elders would gather for a chat. In addition to his own chair, surrounded as it was by a heap of discarded pieces of leather and nails, there would be additional ones for the 'visitors', who would come to discuss a range of topics at a time when television was a thing of the future and radio only available to a few in the village.

Arvonia, the largest shop in the village, sold farming equipment, ships' chandlery, household furniture, paraffin, cartridges, paint, wallpaper and tools of every kind. The shop was started by a William Jones but, when he died, it was run by his son and a daughter, the latter, a very altruistic person, known to everyone as Miss Jones Arvonia, who would buy and distribute books to the children of the village, in addition to anonymously distributing food parcels to the many poor of the village.

The men employed at the Dinorwic Quarry, or on the quay at Port Dinorwic, in the latter part of the nineteenth century, received a wage of between 18/- (90p) and £2 per week. Such an income would barely cover the family's expenditure on rent, food and clothes. When food was short, due to an inadequate wage, a boat would be borrowed for fishing on the Strait. Anything caught could either be eaten by the family or sold and the proceeds used to purchase bread. Wives would also be able to contribute towards the family income by carrying out domestic work for some of the better-off families of the village.

When wages ceased due to illness or unemployment, the only recourse would be to apply for parish relief which amounted to 10/- (50p) a week. Even that would only be considered after a careful assessment by a specially elected Board of Guardians, who would be unlikely to have experienced the trauma and indignity of seeking such assistance at any time of their lives.

When a bereavement occurred, in an attempt to ease the inevitable burden of funeral costs, it was the custom for friends and neighbours to call at the house of the bereaved, not only to sympathise but, also, to take the opportunity of leaving some money or an item such as tea, sugar, butter or bread. This would help towards the refreshments which followed the interment, since many of those attending would have travelled long distances, often on foot.

The first sound to be heard in the village in a working day, would be that of the quarrymen's boots hurrying to catch the six o'clock train from Penscoins which, steamed and ready, conveyed them to Gilfach Ddu, from where they would walk to their allocated place of work somewhere on Elidir mountain, the site of Dinorwic Quarry. Additionally, on Mondays, the Anglesey contingent, who crossed the Menai Strait on the ferry-boat, and who would be staying in the purpose-built barracks at the quarry for the week, would add to the sound.

At 7.30am, the dry-dock whistle would not only announce the start of another working day, but also act as a general alarm for the remainder of the village sleepers. If further early reminders were needed, then there was always the sound of horse-drawn carts selling milk or coal, the postman delivering letters and handcarts laden with locally caught fish or bread and cakes being sold from house-to-house. At nine o'clock, the school bell would chivvy the children, whilst at midday the quay whistle would remind the housewives that the men would soon be home for their dinner. The 1pm whistle would ensure their return for another four hours of work.

The daily trek to the shops for the day's food requirements, presented the women of the village with an opportunity of escaping a very mundane life for an hour or so. Modern devices such as vacuum cleaners and washing machines were virtually unknown in the first part of the twentieth century. The Monday morning ritual of dealing with the washing of the family clothes, was undertaken by lighting a fire under a boiler in an outhouse, irrespective of the weather.

As a result of the main line railway being built and the road down Nant y Garth having to be diverted, the opportunity was taken by G. W. D. Assheton Smith, who had made Vaynol his home, to build the wall round Vaynol park in 1864 and, at the same time, diverting the main road from Bangor to Port Dinorwic, so as to skirt the wall rather than cross his land within the wall (the only way of gaining entry into the park was through one of five lodges, each one occupied by a keeper, the most colourful being Charles Mackenzie who, having been a Pipe Major in the 2nd Bn of the King's Own Scottish Borderers, took up his post in 1893). The isolation of Vaynol within the wall not only kept it private, it also

Charles MacKenzie, lodge keeper and pipe major, c.1894. [Vernon Bowles]

enabled Assheton Smith, in the tradition of the Victorian era, to have a herd of free roaming white cattle, whose temperament was completely unpredictable, alongside a variety of deer and zebras as well as displaying wild animals within cages, possibly for the benefit of his guests.

The cosseted life of the quarry-owner was in complete contrast to the estate workers, whose regimented life allowed little deviation during the working week and virtually none on a Sunday, due to the all-embracing discipline imposed by churches and chapels and also by the Vaynol estate as the main employer.

With the demise of the Vaynol estate and the consequential loss of employment in the 1960s, the character of the delightful village of Felinheli was irrevocably changed. Occupiers of rented Vaynol properties were given the option of buying them, and most did. The dock-side, once occupied by stacked slates awaiting dispatch and regularly replenished by the ubiquitous wooden wagons hauled into place by steam or diesel locomotives, is now occupied by houses. The regular arrival and departure of the slate-carrying vessels has been replaced by smart yachts and cruisers moving silently in and out of the dock. And, since the village is no longer the port of Dinorwic, its name has reverted to Felinheli.

Although the Assheton Smith family had figured largely by name only to most people in Caernarfonshire, since few would have actually set eyes on any member of the family, they would, nevertheless, be altruistically supportive of the many institutions in the county, be it brass or silver bands, choirs, eisteddfods, the local sailing club, hospital funds or even gardening clubs.

1. Travel – Overland and by Ferry

The development of routeways, from primitive or bridle-path beginnings, to roads which could cope with wheeled vehicles, took many years. In north Wales, like many other parts of Britain, roads were slow to be developed as there was little need for them due to a scattered and sparse population. This was particularly true of Caernarfonshire, where roads tended to develop from tracks created between villages by travellers, either on foot or on horseback, passing over private land which, in due course, became easements or a 'right of way' by usage.

When, in 1555, parishes became responsible for maintaining roads within their own boundaries, each able-bodied parishioner was obliged to devote six days a year to roadwork. Inevitably, such an obligation was very unpopular with everyone, particularly as fines could be imposed against the parish if a certain standard of road surface was not maintained. Even if the state of roads within a parish were not up to the standard required by law, it was often felt that they were adequate for the needs of local traffic and, according to the Court of Quarter Sessions records, it would appear that repairs were being carried out reasonably well even in the sixteenth century.

Within the parish of Llanfairisgaer in 1792, individuals who were involved in the statutory road maintenance by providing wagons for transporting materials were John Rowlands, Crûg; Williams Price, Plas Brereton; Robert Williams, Parkia; Thomas Morris, Bryn; William Jones, Tanymaes and Morris Williams, Bodandreg. Others named were William Humphreys and John Edwards, Bush farm; William Rowlands, Tynperthi; Evan Williams, Prysgol; Thomas Williams, Penrallt and Grace Griffiths, Garddfon Inn [PYA 3426].

Those travelling into north Wales and towards Bangor, from the direction of Chester, had to overcome the obstacles of the river Conwy and the mountain at Penmaenmawr, both being considered dangerous. Dr Samuel Johnson recorded in his *Journal of a Journey in Wales 1774*:

> We then came to Conway Ferry, and passed in small boats, with some passengers from the stage coach .... The tide did not serve the large ferry-boat, and therefore our coach could not very soon follow us ....

Richard Fenton described his experience of crossing the Conwy in 1813:

> ... after having our patience tried to the utmost by waiting for about 2 hours at the ferry and experiencing the most unexampled and savage insolence from the ferry man ....

If a successful crossing had been accomplished, a few miles further on, it was necessary to negotiate the mountain at Penmaenmawr. A road, some seven feet wide at its widest, had been cut out of rock and climbed steeply to a height of about 240 feet above sea level. The only protection afforded to vehicles, to prevent them going over the side, was a slight wall, in some places about three feet high, and in others, by a bank about a foot above the road. However, contemporary opinions of the track itself varied considerably, depending no doubt as

Chester–Holyhead Railway, 1849. This view clearly illustrates the dangers inherent in using road transport around Penmaenmawr.
[Science Museum, London]

to whether you were on foot, horseback or attempted it in a horse-drawn vehicle.

A passage in *Tour Through Great Britain*, printed by Straham in 1725, referred to the notorious mountain:

> We went over the famous precipice called Penmaen Mawr which fame has been abundantly more frightful than it really is; it is indeed very high and if any one should fall from it he would be dashed to pieces yet, on the other hand there is no danger of falling and besides there is now a wall built all the way on the edge of the precipice to secure them ....

By 1772, as the result of a Parliamentary grant of £2,000 being given to the Caernarvonshire Old Turnpike Trust, repairs to the notorious Penmaenmawr track allowed travellers a reasonably safe passage. An account written by J. Hemmingway in 1835 about the journey over Penmaenmawr stated:

> This was justly once the dread of the neighbourhood; the immense promontory affording only a narrow zig-zag path along the shelf of its side for the terrified traveller to pass ... even since the new road was cut, namely, on the 31st July 1801 during a tremendous storm of thunder, a mass of stone, supposed to weigh several thousand tons, was loosened from its bed and precipitated with a dreadful crash into the sea ... Before this road was formed, the usual mode of going between Conway and Bangor was either in boats or waiting the departure of the tides to proceed along the sands at low water. The latter mode was frequently attended with danger .... Few carriages at that time were taken betwixt the two towns but nearly all the travellers had to go on horseback ....

The alternative route to the Penmaenmawr road was the Sychnant pass, which would also have been quite formidable, particularly for horse-drawn carriages that were dependent on inadequate braking systems. As a consolation, those who did manage it had the benefit of an inn at each end of the pass with signs that read, on one side:

Before you venture hence to pass
Take a good refreshing glass

and on the other:

Now you're over take another
Your drooping spirits to recover

In an attempt to eliminate the iniquitous costs of maintaining roads at both parish and county level, turnpike trusts were formed in the early part of the eighteenth century. Each trust was given statutory power, usually over a period of 21 years, to maintain certain sections of road to a designated standard and to levy tolls on travellers passing over each section so as to cover costs. Although the toll-gatekeepers, who were responsible for collecting the tolls, had the benefit of a tollhouse, theirs was an onerous task and they had to be on duty day and night each and every day of the year. Inevitably, they bore the resentment of travellers who were very much against the principle of tolls, even though they were intended to be used for improving the condition of the roads (one reason for the Rebecca Riots of 1833–4 in west Wales was the resentment felt against tollgates).

Under the Turnpike Trust legislation, commissioners were allowed to levy what was considered a justifiable toll on road users and these ranged from ¹/₂d. for a farm animal to 4d. for a horse-drawn vehicle. However, this

Sychnant Pass, c.1900. Even at this late date the difficulties of using this road are obvious. [Gwynedd Archives Service]

Left: Llanfairpwll Turnpike with the board still displaying the charges. [Author]

Below: Y Felinheli Turnpike, located just below St Mary's Church. Now demolished. [John Hughes]

Above: Pont Saint, Caernarfon. The old turnpike building can be seen on the far side of the bridge. Now demolished. [Author]

Right: Vaynol turnpike between Bangor ferry and Y Felinheli, c.1970, close to the turning for Penrhosgarnedd. Now demolished. [Bessie Thompson]

latter charge only applied during the months from May to September; between October and April, when the road surface was liable to be damaged by narrow vehicle wheels, the cost was increased to 6d. Having paid their toll to proceed past a turnpike, individuals were allowed to return free of toll, provided it was on the same day with the same horse, cattle or carriage and being in possession of a note or ticket for the respective toll collectors.

Anyone refusing to pay tolls was liable to have any animal, goods or chattels seized and, if the toll remained unpaid, these would be sold within five days, with the difference repaid to the owner. Public stage-coaches had to pay tolls on return journeys, even when they occurred on the same day. Clergy visiting the sick, a funeral being held in another parish, or officers and soldiers carrying material to re-open roads or bridges were allowed to use toll roads free of charge.

Records show that amongst those passing through the Llanrwst tollgate in 1850 were Robert Williams, Penllys and Hugh Hughes, Caeberllan, both transporting slate. They were charged 1/6d for each load if the wagon was being hauled by three horses but, if the load demanded an extra horse, the cost for each trip increased to 2/-. Rather than pay each and every time a lorry load of slate was taken through the Pont Saint tollgate at Caernarfon, Mr Evans of the Cilgwyn Company had made prior arrangements: 'To the Gate Keeper at Pont Saint — I shall pay for the under mentioned Slate Carriers every two months, W. Wyatt will agree to this' [PYA 28482]. As far as Hugh Davies of Trefriw Mill was concerned, he was charged 6d for transporting corn along the toll-road with a cart and one horse (PYA 604). Those who owned toll money were threatened, irrespective of the amount owed:

> You are indebted for tolls at Hendre Turnpike Gate to the amount of £0 7s. 0d. and unless paid to my hand on or before the 10 September instant with 3/6d. costs, proceedings will be commenced against you to enforce payment without further notice. I am, Your Humble Servant, G. Evans, Carnarvon 8 September 1824' [PYA 28485].

When the Caernarvonshire Old Turnpike Trust received its statutory powers in 1769, the first section which it became responsible for was between Tal-y-Cafn and Conwy. From Conwy the new toll road then proceeded through Bangor, Bangor ferry, Caernarfon as far as Pwllheli.

The road between Bangor Ferry and Caernarfon was developed in three stages. The old track from Bangor to Aberpwll and Caernarfon, which had been in existence for many years, was improved with the building of the turnpike road of 1776. From Bangor it passed through Penchwintan, Penrhosgarnedd, Capel Graig and then through land which was subsequently incorporated within the Vaynol wall. As they approached Aberpwll, travellers encountered the first tollhouse near Wern y Gogas, a short distance from a smithy (occupied later by the head gamekeeper for Vaynol and known locally as Parker's lodge). The toll-road then continued through Aberpwll, past the Halfway Inn to the second turnpike at Tafarngrisiau, before continuing across country to Cerrig yr Afon and then on to Caernarfon.

In the second stage of road developments between Bangor and Port Dinorwic (started in 1837), the Wern y Gogas turnpike was moved to the top of Vaynol hill at Capel Graig (the person in residence and responsible for collecting the tolls in 1866 was Hugh Lewis who was described as a subtenant). At the same time, a new post road (Caernarfon Road) extending from Augusta Place was built at Port Dinorwic. This change of route resulted in a new tollgate being built just below the present St Mary's Church, Felinheli.

The third and possibly the most dramatic change occurred with the arrival in 1852 of the London & North Western Railway and its extension to Caernarfon. In anticipation of this, a plan was presented to the court in Caernarfon by Mr Thomas Assheton Smith on 6 November 1851. This outlined that the old road from Nant y Garth, through Siloh, to Four Crosses (Rhiwal) should be diverted to join with the 1837 toll road. This was agreed on the 9 December 1851 by the justices the Rev. James Vincent Vincent and Mr John Vincent Hawksley Williams [GAS XPlan RD 12-1851]. In addition, the main road through the village of Port Dinorwic, instead of proceeding through Augusta Place as hitherto, was diverted to pass beneath the new railway bridge which carried the line to Caernarfon.

The Caernarfonshire tollgate income ranged from £30 at Llanalhaearn to £250 at Pont-y-Saint outside Caernarfon. Other examples were: Gwydir Gate £57; Conwy £95; Penmaenmawr £66; Llandegai £65; Bangor £150 and Tafarn-y-Grisiau (Felinheli) £50. Income at this latter turnpike increased in 1826 to £113 and, in 1840, three years after the road improvements and relocation of the turnpike, to £340. But, possibly as the result of the arrival of the railway, it declined to £160 in 1861 and £125 in 1881. Turnpikes were let annually either by tender or auction, with the income for the previous year being used as a price guide, since income could vary considerably depending on road usage and fees applicable.

By 1838, the 22,000 miles of toll roads in England and Wales controlled by 1,116 Turnpike Trusts, produced an annual income of £1,200,000. Denbighshire Turnpike Trusts ceased to function by around 1865, but the Caernarfonshire Trust continued until 1890 and the Anglesey Trust, which maintained the road from Menai Bridge through Penmynydd and Llangefni to Holyhead, until 1895. Many of the old tollhouses then became private houses but, in the case of the Pont Saint in Caernarfon, this eventually became a little shop selling home made cakes, run by the wife of Harry Thomas, coachman to the Carter family of Bryn Seiont.

The first stage coach to complete the whole journey between London and Holyhead did so in May 1780. The towns which it passed through included Shrewsbury and Llangollen, Corwen, Llanrwst and Conwy. This route enabled travellers to Ireland to avoid the dangerous crossing from Chester and the notorious Conwy ferry. Contemporary reports stated that the overnight stops provided superior accommodation even when compared with that available in Chester. The Penrhyn Arms* in Bangor was described as '… one of the largest and best on the road, with great resources in the way of reception rooms, extensive private suites for the considerable personages who travelled to and from Ireland, and stabling for over a hundred horses …'. The time-keeping of the coaches became so punctual, that clocks and watches would be adjusted in accordance with their arrival and departure [Harper, C. G., *The Holyhead Road*, Vol. II, Chapman & Hall Ltd., 1902].

Even though the Paymaster-General had authorised the Mail-coach to run from Shrewsbury to Menai Bridge ferry for the first time in 1808, a couple of years later, a committee of the House of Commons was appointed to enquire into the state of roads leading to Holyhead, the nearest British port for the crossing to Ireland. Thomas Telford was commissioned to carry out a complete survey and, as a result of which, a parliamentary grant of £20,000 was made available in 1815, in order that he could carry out necessary repairs. In the same year, as part of general improvements and the reduction of travelling time, Telford built the single arch iron bridge over the river Conway at Betws y Coed with its inscription 'This arch was constructed in the same year the battle of Waterloo was fought'.

With increasing traffic on the road between Shrewsbury and Bangor and the inability of the existing six trusts to cope with its repair, they were amalgamated into a new trust called the Shrewsbury–Bangor Ferry Trust with Thomas Telford as its engineer. By 1836, as the result of these improvements and the building of the Menai suspension bridge, at a total cost of £730,000, travelling time between London and Holyhead had been reduced to 27 hours.

* Later to become the original building of the University College of North Wales in 1884, the front porch of which survives at Penlon, Bangor.

Even though the Caernarvonshire Turnpike Trust carried out repairs to the roads leading from Caernarfon into Lleyn, as the result of the 1769 Act, they may well have been very basic in the light of John Wynne's 1861 observations, when he stated that the only means of travelling from Caernarfon in the eighteenth century was either on foot or on horseback. The post was carried on foot from Caernarfon to Bangor, and if prisoners had to be conveyed from the gaol in Caernarfon to London, it was done by ship. When a semblance of road was available, chaise-coaches were used as and when required by travellers, until the 1820s, when a regular service from Caernarfon was developed by an Anthony Dillon (described in trade directories as a seedsman). Conveyance by stage-coach was at best limited to an average speed of twenty-six miles a day [*Hanes Sir a Thre Caernarvon*, John Wynne, 1861].

For the few industries in Caernarfonshire and Anglesey, toll roads were of no benefit since they tended, naturally, to be between towns. As a result, industry during the 18th century remained largely in a parochial state. The possible exception was that of the copper industry of Anglesey, where the entrepreneurial skills of the industrialist Thomas Williams, and the quantity of copper ore being produced at Parys Mountain, had resulted in Anglesey having a virtual monopoly of the world copper market.

By Ferry

Prior to the building of the suspension bridge at Menai Bridge, those who needed to cross the Menai Strait, which separates the Ynys Môn (Anglesey) from the mainland, did so by means of a ferry. Of the six that were available at different points along the strait, the three most important were at Llanfaes, Moel-y-Don (Felinheli), and Porthaethwy (Menai Bridge), the latter being the most frequently used. The other three were at Abermenai (previously described as the Newborough ferry), Porthesgob (the property of the bishops of Bangor) and Caernarfon (Tal y Foel).

At whatever point the traveller decided to cross, there was always an element of danger, especially at night or during adverse weather, as much depended on the skill of ferrymen. Of the six ferries, the most dangerous, due to the distance from the shore to the point where passengers could embark, was the one which operated between Aber and Llanfaes on the outskirts of Beaumaris. To gain access to the ferry, which had been operating since Edward I granted a lease to Beaumaris, it was necessary for passengers to walk across the Lavan Sands to a point where there was sufficient water for the ferry to take them on board.

E. Hyde Hall in his description of the crossing commented:

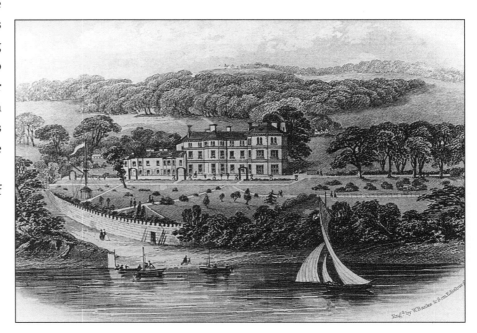

Bangor ferry and the George Hotel, c.1820 (now part of the University College buildings). [Gwynedd Archives Service]

The turnpike road runs for about three miles through the parish in a south-westerly direction. Hence also is carried a short road to the beach, from which at low water a passage is obtained across the (Lavan) sands to the ferry at Beaumaris...These sands, soft and dirty as they are in places, are at all times unpleasant and sometimes dangerous, and to guide the wayfarer in foggy or dark weather the church bell is sometimes tolled or a light exposed ... .

To alleviate some of the danger to would-be travellers, an order was made in 1778, that poles had to be provided across the sands at regular intervals, indicating the route to be taken to get to

Above: The Min-y-Don ferry hut at Port Dinorwic with passengers waiting to be taken across to Anglesey, c.1920. [Marjorie Harris]

Right: Waiting for passengers at Moel-y-Don, Anglesey. [Port Dinorwic Historical Society]

Below: A grossly over-laden ferry carrying slate quarrymen returning to Anglesey at midday Saturday. [Gwynedd Archive Service]

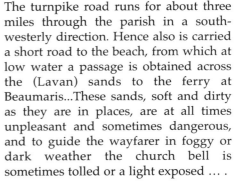

the point where the ferry could be boarded for the trip to Beaumaris.

The Moel-y-Don ferry, which had been in existence since 1608, was considered the safest since it was less affected by tide and wind when compared to the Tal-y-Foel to Caernarfon ferry. However, such an opinion was at variance with a report in *The Carnarvon & Denbigh Herald* of 13 October 1893:

Moel-y-Don, one passenger arriving and others awaiting embarkation for the short journey to Port Dinorwic, c.1910. [Port Dinorwic Historical Society]

The boats are semi-coracles and leaking. There is a rude stone jetty on the Anglesey side. But what about the accommodation for waiting passengers especially in boisterous weather? On the Carnarvonshire side there is a ... licensed place (Garddfon Inn) where people may seek shelter ... the Anglesey Temperance Association (should) spend some of the money it collects (for) shelters on the Anglesey side of Moel-y-Don where hundreds of Llanberis quarrymen cross weekly. (Ed. note ... should not the Woods and Forest Department ... provide accommodation worthy of the 19th century).

It would appear that describing the ferry-boats as 'semi-coracles' was an exaggeration since, not only did the ferries carry people, they were also capable of carrying sheep, pigs, goats and dairy produce from Anglesey for sale on the mainland. At the time when the Port Dinorwic slate quay was being extended and further land being reclaimed from the sea in 1853–4, the opportunity was taken to move the jetty used by the ferry from a position directly at the bottom of Snowdon Street to its present position near the Garddfon Inn.

Prior to the introduction of the motorised ferry at Moel y Don, boats of 18–20 feet were rowed across to and from Moel-y-Don, assisted, when the conditions were favourable, by a mainsail. Quarrymen living on Anglesey needing to catch the train from Port Dinorwic to Llanberis would have to start from their homes in the early hours of Monday morning because of the distance involved, so as to get to the ferry by 4am. To shorten the distance from home to shore, some of the quarrymen would arrange to be picked up at Trefarthin or Porthamal, instead of Moel-y-Don, at an additional charge of 1d. If the number of quarrymen on board was large, especially on a Monday morning or Saturday afternoon, it was not unusual for extra oars to be brought into use and a passenger or two asked to assist. The ferry ran on a regular basis throughout the day, but was particularly busy in the early morning when vendors brought their wares to sell at Port Dinorwic, either from a stall near the jetty, or from handcarts pushed from house to house.

There have been a number of individuals from Felinheli associated with the ferry in the latter part of the nineteenth century and in the first

Moel-y-Don ferry arriving from Port Dinorwic, c.1950. [Port Dinorwic Historical Society]

Moel-y-Don ferry, named Conway, *1907. [Vernon Bowles]*

half of the twentieth century including John Owen (1852), John Williams (1874), Richard Williams (1877) and William Owen (1897). They were followed by Captain William Williams, who leased the ferry from 5 April 1912 until 1920 at a cost of £47 per annum.* Others who were involved in its running at different periods were Robert Caddock, Thomas Henry Williams (Vaults Bach), Harry Jones Roberts and Thomas Lillie. The three boats involved were the *Conway*, the *Great Orme* and the 28-foot *Menai* which was the first motorised ferry-boat to be used at Moel-y-Don.

When the service was being run jointly between Thomas Lillie and Harry Jones Roberts, they used the boats already mentioned together with the *Betty* (built by Matthew Owen at Menai Bridge) and Nancy, which was used as a stand-by. When Lillie's operating lease expired in 1935 it was not renewed until 1938, when it was run by Arthur Roberts with a boat called *Arvona* (also built by Matthew Owen). The renewal of the lease in 1938 coincided with the Crown rights to the ferry being conveyed to the Anglesey and Caernarfonshire County Councils for the sum of £50. Karl Petrel, Hugh Dop and Eric Owen each ran the ferry for a period before it was taken over by Eddie Owen.

The post-First World War period, with its greater choice of buses and increasing number of individuals

*He commanded a mine-sweeper during the First World War.

Garth ferry at the Gazelle Inn, Anglesey. [Gwynedd Archives Service]

owning private cars, saw a decline in the use being made of the ferry. The trips across the strait were mostly for recreational reasons rather than business usage (with the possible exception of people living in the vicinity of Moel-y-Don coming to carry out shopping at Felinheli). A trip on the ferry, so as to enjoy a picnic and a swim on the Anglesey sands at the time of the summer school holiday, was always a pleasant experience. Inevitably, with such reduced patronage, the ferry would

Garth ferry at the Gazelle Inn, Anglesey. [Author]

only operate for two hours a day, if at all, during the winter. In addition to a wage of £4 paid by the councils, the ferryman was allowed to retain the 3d return fare which passengers were charged. Out of this meagre income he had to pay for the running of the 20-foot open motor-boat.

Although the public transport that became available in the 1920s was very basic by today's standards, it nevertheless provided an alternative means of transport for those who had relied on the ferry service, affected as it was by both weather and tidal conditions. By comparison, the buses provided a regular and reliable service with a variety of routes to choose from.

By 1958, the Caernarfonshire and Anglesey County Councils decided that, because of the diminishing number of passengers using the ferry, it was not considered economically viable to continue with the service even during the summer months.

Even after the Menai Suspension Bridge had been built in 1826, people living in the southern part of Anglesey continued to trade in Caernarfon, as had been the custom for many years. For those living in villages adjacent to the Menai Strait, a trip across to Caernarfon entailed a comparatively short walk down to Tan y Foel, where they would catch the ferry known as *'stemar bach Sîr Fôn'*. Youngsters living in Anglesey furthering their education in Caernarfon during the latter part of the nineteenth and the early part of the twentieth centuries, would also make use of the ferry. The time of departure was scheduled for 8.30am, but its arrival at Caernarfon would depend on a number of factors, not least the weather and the state of the tide. At least pupils had the benefit of a good excuse if they arrived late at school, which they often did, especially during the winter months. The ferry trip across the Strait was something of an adventure, with the vagaries of the weather adding to the excitement as compared to travelling in a rickety bus, when they became available in the 1920s, over the Menai Suspension Bridge.

Additional trips on the Strait were available, as an advertisement in a local paper in the early part of the 20th century stated:

Caernarvon & Anglesey Ferry — daily service to and from Anglesey by well equipped motor-boats. Parties specially catered for. Frequent trips along the Menai Straits and to Llanddwyn Lighthouse. All particulars from Borough Surveyor, Guild Hall, Caernarvon.

Ferry boats used in the latter days of service between Bangor pier and Beaumaris were the *Mary Ann*, *Mona*, *Sarah*, *Dumpy*, *Cynfal*, *Torbay*, *Nantllys* and *Lady Magdallen* with its twin screw engine. The latter boat, under the charge of Robert Hughes, who was also a Menai Strait pilot by profession, occasionally took passengers on an evening excursion from Bangor to Caernarfon and back at a cost of 5/- per person.

In addition to the 'official' Corporation ferry which operated between Caernarfon and Tal-y-Foel in Anglesey, additional ferries were also being run wherever and whenever there was a demand, especially if it saved passengers from a lengthy walk or ride by horse and cart. In the early part of the 19th century, such a ferry operated between Tal-y-Foel and Plas Brereton until 1837 when it ran from Tal-y-Foel to Waterloo Port. People who lived on Anglesey, particularly those whose homes bordered the Strait, commuted regularly to the mainland by means of the ferry.

2 – Shipbuilding and Transport of Goods

Shipbuilding

The condition of the roads in north Wales, certainly in the eighteenth century, inhibited the development of industry and the movement of merchandise, whether they were intended for export or home use. The alternative was to continue using sea transport. The North Wales Port Book 1725–30 (covering Beaumaris, Conwy, Pwllheli, Caernarfon and Holyhead) list the cargoes carried as barley, herrings, bricks, oranges, timber, hops, bacon, paving stones and Irish horses [UCNW Bangor 484].

The increasing export of slate during the period 1770–1890 corresponded with a similar increase in ship-building along the north Wales coast. This not only created a need for craftsmen in the ship-yards and crews for the ships, but also provided an alternative to being employed on the land or in the slate quarries.

The ships, which were built by local craftsmen in Caernarfonshire during the latter part of the eighteenth and the greater part of the nineteenth centuries, were generally small sloops whose tonnage ranged from a mere 7 tons to larger vessels of 400 tons. The number built at the three leading ship-building yards were 446 at Pwllheli (total tonnage of 30,400); Porthmadog and Borth-y-Gest 253 (total tonnage of 27,000) and Caernarfon 203 (total tonnage of 12,600). The figures available for 1866 give an indication as to whether these and other vessels built along the coast were registered at Beaumaris or Caernarfon:

> under 50 tons — Beaumaris 132 (4,356 tons), Caernarfon 170 (5,722 tons).
> over 50 tons — Beaumaris 166 (14,979 tons), Caernarfon 363 (37,757 tons).

Grampus, a brigantine of 132 tons and measuring 88' 6" x 22' 5" x 12' 1", was built by John Roberts in 1859 at Bangor and sold to John Millington, Bryntirion, Vaenol in 1860 with John Jones acting as his agent and William Bodelly Buckingham of Port Dinorwic acting as his accountant. Trade directories list at least three other shipyards at Bangor: Henry Owen and Elizabeth Roberts who are described as ship and boat builders; T. T. Parry, who had a patent slip and 'all requisite appliances for repairing ships, ship-smith etc' at Garth Point, and Samuel Roberts, a boat builder, ship chandler and sail-maker in Strand Street, Hirael.

The people who lived in the hamlet of Dinas, later to become part of Port Dinorwic, had been involved in the maintenance and building of wooden-hulled ships for a period of over a hundred years — c.1780–1900. Vessels that were built there in the latter part of the eighteenth century were the *Earl of Uxbridge* (brig) 120 tons (1783); *Little John* (sloop) 13 tons (1783); *Lady Caroline* (sloop) 40 tons (1786); *Betsy* (sloop) 19 tons (1786); *Nancy* (sloop) 12 tons (1789) and *Countess of Uxbridge* (brig) 19 tons (1791). They were used in carrying slate from the developing village to ports mostly along the north Wales coast, returning with general cargo.

In the nineteenth century, Dinas shipyard, trading as Rees Jones & Son, Shipwrights, was owned and managed by the Rev. Rees Jones, a Methodist minister and a native of Barmouth, who lived at nearby Glan Menai, and his son, William E. Jones. Having had experience in ship-building at Borthwen on the river Mawddach in the early 40s, his Port Dinorwic workforce numbered between 30–40 people including carpenters, smiths, sail-makers and labourers, creating a weekly wage bill of between £30 and £50, but peaking at 80 men, possibly with the construction of the *Ordovic* in 1877. Their reputation for both design and quality of construction, encouraged other shipbuilders, such as William Thomas from Liverpool, to seek the advice of Rees Jones and his son on many maritime matters.

Worrall's Trade Directory for 1871 described the shipyard as 'having a patent slip and all appliances for repairing ships and block and mast makers, ship smiths etc'. *Slater's Trade Directory* for Port Dinorwic listed R. & W. Jones as sail-makers and ships' chandlers and noted also that Jane Jones (trading as Halfway Stores at The Halfway Inn —licensee Owen Owens) was listed as as a shipsmith. The same directory indicated that the Harbour Master at the port was John Hughes.

In addition to being a shipbuilder, W. E. Jones was also involved with the Gwynedd Shipping Company (based at Glandŵr, Clwt-y-Bont, Caernarfonshire) which owned the *Moel Tryfan* (80241)* a four masted barque of 1,639 tons. She had been built by William Doxford & Sons of Sunderland in 1884. On her maiden voyage to Singapore, with a general cargo, she was under the command of Captain John Williams of Newborough, who had served with local ships mostly concerned in the export of slate. In 1901, as a result of ballast shifting during heavy weather when travelling through the English Channel, she capsized and sank 25 miles west of the Caskets. Of the crew of eighteen, twelve were lost including the captain, Evan Jones of Frongoch, Caernarfon. The six survivors were taken to Cherbourg by a French fishing vessel.

The shipbuilding industry at Port Dinorwic enjoyed a well-deserved reputation for the quality of its work, and wealthy individuals, by buying a certain number of shares in a vessel as an investment, would in effect advance money for its construction and operation and, in return, shared in any profit that the vessel eventually made. The proportion of capital invested to the total cost of the vessel would be indicated by the number of shares held from a maximum of sixty-four. The opportunity to invest in a vessel would usually be advertised in local papers or by means of posters:

> To be sold by auction at the Crown Tavern in the town of Caernarvon on Friday the 12th day of September 1823 between the hours of three and five o'clock in the afternoon...Six Sixtyfourth parts or shares of that new, strong built and fast Sailing Smack called the Carnarvon Packet of the Port of Carnarvon Burthen pre-register 53 2/94 tons. Griffith Jones — Late Master [PYA 31044].

Amongst those Port Dinorwic businessmen with entrepreneurial skills who participated in such an investment was John T. Jones, the one time manager of the Vaenol Estate who lived at Terfyn Terrace (which he had built from ballast stones brought by local ships from Scottish ports) who owned the *Lady Lisgar*, the *Abyssinia* and the *Marathon*, all crewed by local sailors. Captain Owen Davies, also a resident of Terfyn Terrace, had two large ships, the *Athena* and the *Florence Brackington*, which were commanded by his two sons, Owen and David.

Although they were no longer being used for carrying general cargo, the old wooden hulled coasters which had served the area so well for many years, continued working by carrying building materials for the houses in the developing village of Felinheli in the first half of the nineteenth century. *Virtue* and *Neptune* were two such boats which were taken across to the Anglesey shore where they were loaded with sand and stone.

---

*The Lloyd's Shipping Register number.

Drawing of the Ordovic, *built at Dinas, Y Felinheli, 1877. [Alun Lewis Jones]*

Ordovic (74874)

Of the twenty-nine vessels built at Port Dinorwic by the firm of Rees Jones & Son during the nineteenth century, the shipyard had the distinction of building the 853 tons *Ordovic* the largest vessel to be built in north Wales. Registered at Caernarfon and described as a three-masted barque with an elliptic stern and of carvel construction (that is each plank placed on top of each other rather than in the clinker style where planks overlapped each other), the *Ordovic* measured 168.8 x 33.8 x 21.3 feet and work started on the barque on 28 March 1875. The 64-part share in the vessel was divided between: Rees Jones 19/64; William Edward Jones 25/64; Griffith Davies, Dolgellau 2/64; Hugh Hughes, Dolgellau 2/64; Griffith Griffiths, Llanbedr 6/64; William Hughes, Amlwch 5/64 and Jane Davies and Mary Evans, Menai Bridge 5/64.

The launching of ships at Port Dinorwic must have been a regular village occurrence, nevertheless, when it came to the launching of such a large vessel as the *Ordovic*, it was an event that was not going to be missed by anyone and especially the children, as is obvious from the log-book entry by the headmaster of the local school:

> 2 March. There was a holiday on Wednesday – the brig *Gordovic*.* [sic] In giving the afternoon as well as morning, I have escaped the risk of having to punish in all probability about half the children for non-attendance which at present might have proved injurious.

The *Cambrian News* of 9 March 1877 describing the scene on the day of the launch of the *Ordovic* stated:

> The launching operations were carried on with much 'eclat', the key wedge was struck off by Mrs Wyn-Griffith, Llanfair Hall, and as soon as the blow had struck, the huge vessel made a steady start, and in a few seconds she was floating leisurely on the middle of the Menai Straits, in the care of her future conductor, Captain Joseph Richardson (he had already served as Captain of the Atlanta, another of Rees Jones' ships launched in 1864).

After two years work and to celebrate the successful launch, the builders organised a dinner for specially invited guests aboard the floating vessel — but before the masts and rigging had been installed. This was followed by a dinner for those who had been involved in the actual construction.

Accompanying 48-year old Captain George Richardson on its maiden voyage was William Roberts (Mate) and Griffith Richards (2nd Mate). Due to its size, the *Ordovic* could accommodate 28 men, but the regularly produced crew list showed a considerable turnover in manpower. Although some members of the original crew were recruited from Port Dinorwic or nearby towns, records indicate that there was tendency for the Welsh crew to be discharged and her crew to became more cosmopolitan, having been recruited from a variety of countries including Malta, Denmark (Copenhagen) and Prussia. In 1864, a 16-year old 'boy' sailor could expect to be paid £1 5s. 0d. per month, an able seaman £3 per month and a carpenter £6 per month.

---

* Correction in the margin: Ordovic (not Gordovic) being launched.

David Pierce memorial card. [Nancy Pierce]

The first voyage, in the April following the launch, was to Cardiff where the ship was loaded with coal bound for Batavia. One member of the crew, who was experiencing his first voyage as ship's carpenter and earning £6 per month, was 35-year-old David Pierce from Port Dinorwic. Another crew member from the village, voyaging for the first time, was 18-year old David Owens. On their ship's arrival at Cardiff, the records indicate that David Pierce was discharged but no reason was recorded.

The *Ordovic* sailed to Greenock on 22 February 1877, where the remaining crew from Port Dinorwic were discharged. When she sailed to Antwerp on 6 August 1880, her crew included men from France, Finland, Denmark, Germany, Belgium and Sweden. The captain's report for 31 August 1880 stated that Charles Tealking, AB, had died of dysentery. Her next voyage, with Captain Richardson still in command, was from London to Yokohama, departing on 11 November 1880 and calling at India, China, Australia, New Zealand and Japan, before crossing to America and the West Indies. She arrived back in Britain on 9 June 1882.

When Captain Richardson was nearly sixty years of age, he retired from the *Ordovic* and his successor was the twenty-eight-year old Captain Evan Jones from Pwllheli, who was in command when the *Ordovic* sailed on 18 February 1886, on a voyage that was to take her via Valparaiso and India to Sydney, Australia, returning to Britain by 17 August 1887. For some of the crew, the voyage was but a short one as a note 'discharged at Dunkirk' appears against certain names, including the following who were from Port Dinorwic: William Roberts, aged 23, carpenter, paid £5 per month; Rees Jones Williams, aged 18, able seaman, paid £1 5s. and John Jones, aged 18, able seaman, paid £1 5s. per month. Against the name of Robert Williams, aged 21, able seaman, who was paid £1 7s. 6d. per month was marked the note 'deserted Newcastle'.

With rising costs and the bank Williams & Co., of Caernarfon pressing for a loan to be repaid, W. E. Jones decided that the time had come to sell the *Ordovic,* which he managed to do on 7 March, 1888, for £1,600 to a John Austin of Swansea, with Thomas Austin, possibly the new owner's son, taking command. She left Cardiff on 14 May 1894 but, sadly, was wrecked at Pascagoula, Cape Horn, on 9 October. There does not appear to be any record of the fate of the crew who were, by that time, mostly from south Wales and the Continent.

By the end of the nineteenth century, the demand for wooden hulled ships diminished and this once thriving industry at Dinas suddenly ceased in 1897. The Dinas community was further affected when the nearby slate works also closed and the workforce amalgamated with its counterpart at Old Station near the Halfway Inn. (See Appendix II for a list of ships built by Rees Jones & Son.)

Transport of goods

During the eighteenth and nineteenth centuries, hundreds of small vessels traded between the various ports along the north Wales coast and across the Irish sea. The *Golden Apple* of Red Wharf Bay would deliver herrings to Dublin and barley and oats for Liverpool, returning to Beaumaris with coal, salt, tobacco and candles. The *Slive of Bardsey* carried potatoes from Lleyn to Barmouth, and butter, cheese and barley to Liverpool, returning with salt and iron. Similar vessels would also deliver farm produce, grain, eggs, butter and cheese to the larger towns, returning with a cargo of limestone which, after processing, would be used as fertilizer on the land. As a result of increasing agricultural output in Lleyn during the latter half of the eighteenth century, the opportunity was taken to export some of the produce, including wheat and potatoes, through the port of Pwllheli.

Since it was virtually impossible to transport goods over land in north Wales until the latter part of the eighteenth century, such was the availability of ships and frequency of service, goods and passengers continued to be carried by small coastal vessels, such as the *Prince Fredrick William, Roma* and *Christiana*, between Liverpool and ports on the north Wales coast, until the early part of the twentieth century. Whenever possible, a cargo would be discharged as near as possible to the point where it was required, as was the case when Plas Llanfaglan fields at Caernarfon needed to be treated, manure would be brought across from Ireland in a small schooner, with Owen Owen, Sarn, as skipper, and beached at nearby Porth Lleidiog, in order that the cargo could be unloaded directly on to a number of horse-drawn carts. When the competitive railway system was introduced to north Wales in the middle of the nineteenth century, it provided a reliable and safe service since it was not affected by adverse weather and tidal conditions as were the ships. Even so, coastal trade continued for a further fifty years or more.

During the nineteenth century, improvements were carried out to the Caernarfon harbour enabling slates to be exported to Liverpool, Bristol and Dublin and nearly 1,000 tons of copper ore, brought by horse-drawn wagons from Nantlle to Caernarfon Quay, were exported in 1844. Caernarfon's main imports *c.*1834 were timber from the American colonies, wine, coal and groceries.

Although the coastal vessels, many of which had been built along the coast which they served, were invariably small, they were still capable of carrying a steady supply of slate from Porthmadog, Caernarfon, Port Dinorwic and Bangor to ports round the coast of Britain and even to the continent. As demand for slate grew, so did the need for larger vessels and better harbours with improved loading facilities. When the new harbour at Port Dinorwic was completed in 1900, the non-tidal lock system, the only one of its kind in north Wales, enabled vessels to move easily within the port, thereby facilitating the loading of slate.

With many hundreds of ships of varying sizes plying along the north Wales coast, carrying an assortment of cargoes for various destinations, it became imperative that a form of communication be established in order that their movement could be monitored. It was for this reason that the Liverpool Dock Trust established, in 1826, a system of semaphore stations at intervals between Liverpool and Holyhead, a distance of 80 miles, which continued in use until 1860.

An individual, with entrepreneurial skills, who realised that there was a large retail market waiting to be developed in north Wales, was David Jones who started as a shopkeeper at Llandderfel in the 1850s and, by reinvesting his profits in a wide variety of goods, soon had a thriving business. Amongst his many skills was the ability to dispense simple drugs at a time when there was a paucity of doctors in the county. The business, which he sold in 1862, had thrived due to the reputation he had established for quality of goods and reliability of service.

When he subsequently went into partnership in Liverpool to form the firm of David Jones & Co., he used the shipping company firm of Robert Owen and Company of 28 Brunswick Road, Liverpool which, according to the Lloyd's Register, traded as the Aberdovey and Barmouth Steamship Company, for the conveyance and distribution of the company goods along the north Wales coast.

Vessels used by this company were the 71 ton *Jane Jones*, 67' in length, built at Aberdovey in 1857 and the similar size *Quarry Maid,* also built in Aberdovey in 1859. Built by Fullertons of Paisley, the steam vessels *Telephone, Rebecca* and *Countess of Lisburne,* were also used along the north Wales coast. The latter vessel ran a weekly service with general cargo to the Menai Strait calling at Beaumaris, Bangor, Menai Bridge, Pwllfanog, Port Dinorwic and Caernarfon, in addition to a weekly trip to Aberystwyth.

The 259 ton *Christiana,* named after Miss Christiana Roberts, the daughter of a partner in the company, was also built at Paisley in 1896 at a cost of £5,456 19s. 10d. She carried a varied cargo, twice weekly, from Liverpool to the Menai Strait calling at Beaumaris, Bangor, Menai Bridge, Pwllfanog, Port Dinorwic, Caernarfon, Porthdinllaen, Pwllheli and Porthmadog. In the latter part of the nineteenth and early part of the twentieth centuries, she carried a crew of eight under the command of Captain Griffiths, with Jeremiah Davies as Mate. Such was the regularity of her visits to Port Dinorwic, that a quayside shed was known as '*Sied Christiana*' and this is where her delivered cargo would be stored until required by the local shopkeepers. *Christiana* also had the unfortunate experience of cutting Bangor pier in half during a storm in the winter of 1914.

The SS *Dora,* also built in 1896, traded weekly with Porthdinllaen, Barmouth and Aberdovey. At Porthdinllaen, she would discharge her cargo, depending on the stage of the tide, either at Cei Dora or, if necessary, by beaching her so allowing goods to be loaded directly on to horse-drawn carts. Captain David Williams, Llysalaw, Morfa Nevin was in command of the *Dora* running between Aberdovey and Liverpool, until she was sunk by a German U-boat off the Mull of Galloway in 1917 [UCNW 11542].

The steamer *Prince Ja Ja,* one of the many ships built by William Thomas of Amlwch, was owned by the Liverpool, Caernarvon & Menai Straits Steamship Company and crewed by local men (long serving members of the crew and their families would invariably be given the tag 'Ja Ja' after their names).This vessel left West Side, Trafalgar Dock, Liverpool every Wednesday with goods bound for Beaumaris, Caernarfon and Bangor and every Saturday for Menai Bridge and Caernarfon [*C&DH*, 10.3.1883]. She would carry grain from Liverpool for Morris & Jones which would be discharged at Bangor the 'Ja Ja Jetty' (as it was known) in Bangor. From there the grain would be taken for processing at a local mill and sold in packets designated Snowdon Flake Self-Raising Flour.

The firm of Morris & Jones Ltd, was founded in 1865 by Edward Morris, who shipped goods from Liverpool to the port of Mostyn in Flintshire, from where it would be transported by horse and cart along the coast. In an attempt to introduce an alternative form of transport for the firm's products and, at the same time, improve the service to their customers, David Jones & Co. introduced in 1912 steam traction engines built by Fodens of Sandbach, at a cost varying between £658 and £1,155. These 'Dreadnoughts' (as they were called) were capable of carrying 3 tons as compared to the 'Sarahs' maximum capacity of 5 tons. The first engines, which were originally dark green in colour (but were later changed to red), were used until the outbreak of the First World War, when they were commandeered and sent to France with their volunteer drivers. On their return in 1918, to enable various advertisements such as 'Golden Stream Tea' to be displayed prominently on the side, the colour was changed to yellow. These engines, frequently seen travelling though Caernarfonshire towns and villages, were never popular due to the quantity of smoke being emitted and the trail of red hot cinders left along the streets. Even though the speed of these smoking monsters did not exceed 5 m.p.h., their steel wheels caused severe skidding problems, especially during the winter months, when it was not unusual for them to be stuck in snowdrifts for days at a time.

In 1922, the firm of Morris & Jones Ltd. became established in Caernarfon, when it took over the business of Lake & Company which had two shops in Bridge Street. Goods delivered by the *Cristo* and *Virtually* were able to discharge their cargo directly into the Morris & Jones warehouse alongside the quay at Caernarfon. Other ships used for deliveries were *Hatchmere, Redesmere, Roma, Alexander, Penrhyn* and *George* (the latter was sunk during the Second World War when it hit a mine). With more and more goods being brought by rail rather than by sea, unloading at Caernarfon could be done just as easily from the railway wagon directly into the same nearby warehouse. The two firms of David Jones & Co. and Morris & Jones Ltd. amalgamated in 1959 to form Mace Marketing Services.

Industry in Anglesey and Caernarfonshire during the latter half of the eighteenth and the first half of the nineteenth century was largely confined to agriculture, slate, copper and lead.

3. Road and Rail Crossings

The Menai Suspension Bridge

As early as the sixteenth century, Robin Ddu of Bangor had prophesised that a bridge would have to be built across the Menai Strait at some time in the future. By the late eighteenth century, ways of bridging the Strait had been under discussion for many years, but there had always been objections to any plan submitted, the main one being the possibility of interference with the passage of ships along the Strait.

On 1 October, 1783 a 'List of Subscribers' was being compiled towards defraying the expense of:

> … an application to the Parliament of England to make an embankment or dam with a lock and drawbridge over and a Cross or Arm of the Sea between the Counties of Anglesey and Carnarvon called the Streights of Menei and a new road thro' certain lands on each side of the said Embankment in order to open a communication with the Great Road leading from England to Ireland etc. [UCNW, Plas Newydd MSS, 2450].

The opposition to the embankment became organised at a public meeting held at Caernarfon on 9 December 1783, when a committee was formed under the title 'Committee for the Navigation of the Straits of Menai' with Lord Newborough, Lord Penrhyn and Mr Thomas Assheton Smith as the main objectors. It was stated that the underlying objections to changes appeared to be the supposition that Anglesey gentry might gain at the expense of those on the mainland.

In January 1784, William Jessop put forward a plan to build a wooden bridge at Cadnant, but the Parliamentary Bill promoting the scheme was not proceeded with. Opposition generally continued as was reported 11 March 1784 that "… the Carnarvonshire gentry are determined to oppose any plan to build a bridge at Bangor Ferry," [UCNW Plas Newydd MSS 2453] even though a report by two engineers stated on the 2 April 1785 "… that a bridge as is visualised will in no way injure the navigation of the Straits [UCNW, Plas Newydd MSS, 2455]. The practical objections raised were probably based upon the increasing use of the Strait by vessels carrying slates. Possibly because of a business connection at Parys Mountain, Thomas Williams of Llanidan reported to Lord Uxbridge on 21 March, 1786:

> … counsel heard on the Menai Bridge Bill … The whole House was convinced of the impracticality of the Scheme as well as the dangerous consequences that must result to the navigation of the Straits [UCNW, Plas Newydd MSS, 2459].

It appears that the lack of progress being made with the Menai bridge project during 1785–6 was also due to the Caernarfon gentry being prejudiced against it because of their fears that Bangor might benefit at their expense.

Even though seemingly influential individuals continued to object to the proposals, the engineer John Rennie was asked to survey the Menai Strait in 1800 and prepare designs on behalf of the Government. He submitted two plans. One was for three cast iron arches, each with a span of 350 feet and 150 feet above high water, and the other of a single arch, with a span of 450 feet and 150 feet high in the centre, above Ynys Moch. The estimated cost of the former was £290,417 and the latter £31,000 less. Again, there was opposition to any form of bridge across the Strait, with the Caernarvon Harbour Trust petitioning against it on 3 March, 1802 stating that '… as the proposed bridge will injure the interest of the Right Honourable Lord Boston in Moel y Don and Tan y Foel ferries, that their Lordships be requested to use their influence against the Bill …'. A further ten years were to elapse before Thomas Telford was asked to submit his design.

The Nags Head Coffee Room, Carnarvon (1802 annual subscription £1 1s. 0d.) was the place where the élite of the town gathered to discuss news of the proposed bridge to be built across the Menai Strait and ways of objecting to it. Some of the subscribers named were: O. A. Poole, William Griffith, Edmund Crawley, Thomas Jones (surgeon), Zacheus Jones, William Robyns, Edward Cheshire, Robert Currie and Matthew Fleming. In an attempt to raise the profile of the place a letter was sent to Lord Anglesey on 30 March, 1802: '… I beg to know, as soon as convenient, whether I may add your Name thereto (as a member) …' [PN1632-II].

Edmund Hyde Hall, writing in 1810 and possibly commenting on Rennie's design, stated:

> The projected bridge is to be thrown across the Swilly [sic] rocks with three vast iron arches one hundred and fifty feet above high water mark, and connected with the land on each side by a succession of smaller arches. The completion of such work would certainly give to Europe one of its most magnificent ornaments.

No further progress was made until Thomas Telford was commissioned by the Lords of the Treasury in 1810, *inter alia*, as to the best method of bridging the Strait. The report submitted by him the following year included two plans: one at the Swelly Rock and the other at Ynys Moch, with the latter being recommended by him at an estimated cost of £127,331. Neither plan was deemed suitable, since they did not conform with the Admiralty's directive that any structure had to be 100 feet above high water level. Having had these designs rejected, Telford was instructed to consider a similar design to his proposal for a suspension bridge at Runcorn. This brief was for two bridges, one over the river Conwy and the other over the Menai Strait, the latter having to comply with the Admiralty's demands. To accomplish such a requirement, the plans submitted by Telford in 1817 were in the form of a suspension bridge with two main piers, one on the Caernarfon shore and the other on Ynys y Moch on the Anglesey side. In addition, the design allowed for three arches to be built on the Caernarfon side and four on the Anglesey side.

The 579 foot span between the two piers, suspended on 16 chains, carried dual carriageways each 12 feet wide together with a 6 foot wide footpath between the two roadways. A parliamentary grant of £123,000 was approved in 1818 for the bridge to be built at Ynys Moch, the narrowest part of the Strait,

Thomas Telford (1758–1834). [Courtesy British Museum]

The Menai suspension bridge. [Author]

where, for centuries, cattle, brought across Anglesey by drovers, had been swum across, even though the passage was fraught with danger.

The first stone, three tons in weight, of the Menai Suspension Bridge was laid on the 10 August, 1819 and this forms part of the pier on Ynys Moch. Labourers were paid 1/8d. to 2/- per day, increasing to 4/- per day for a foreman. Carpenters and smiths each received a daily wage of 3/6d. Captains of vessels, such as the *Sally* and *Swansea*, transporting the dressed stone from Penmon, were paid between 2/6d. and 4/6d. per day. Those workers who had to suffer working in water at the base of the piers were rewarded with ale but, if the weather

Menai suspension bridge with toll gates and a speed restriction of 4mph or walking pace, c.1924. [Author]

was particularly bad, they were supplied with spirits. In nine days during December 1819, 52 gallons of ale were consumed by these men. It took four years for the masonry work, including the series of limestone piers and arches to be completed, ready to receive the chains which weighed nearly 2,200 tons.

In order to facilitate the raising of the sixteen chains into position from rafts, the Admiralty authorised the Strait to be closed to shipping. The first chain was raised on 26 April, 1825 with the aid of two capstans operated by 150 labourers. The last one was in position by 9 July, 1825 and the bridge opened to traffic in January 1826* Following a severe gale in January 1839 and the subsequent repairs carried out to the structure during 1839–40, the weight of the bridge was increased by 130 tons to a figure of 774 tons which amounted to a strain on the main chains of 5 tons per square inch.

When the manner of crossing the Strait by steam trains was under consideration, a report presented by Admiral F. Beaumont on 4 November, 1836 stated that:

> … if railroad should be constructed for that purpose…it is not likely that a steam carriage with a loaded train would be allowed to traverse the present chain bridge (Menai Bridge) at Bangor …

When it was realised that such an arrangement would be totally impractical, since the bridge could not sustain such an additional weight, there was no alternative but to build an additional bridge if the railway was to continue to Holyhead.

The £123,000 grant for the construction of the bridge was repaid by applying tolls at the following rates:

1.	State and Mail Coaches	2/-
2.	Post Chaise, Coach, Landau, Berlin, Barouche and Chaise with four wheels and four horses	3/-
3.	Ditto with two horses	2/-
4.	Chaise, Chair or Gig with two wheels	6d.
5.	Waggon, Wain, Cart etc with four wheels	1/-
6.	Ditto with two wheels	6d.
7.	Horse, Mule, Ass not drawing any carriage	2d.
8.	Foot passenger	1d.
9.	Drove of oxen, cows or cattle per score	1/-
10.	Drove of Hogs, calves, sheep or lambs per score	6d.

Tolls for crossing the Menai Suspension Bridge continued to be paid from 1826 until 1940, when the structure was strengthened by replacing the wrought iron with steel, and weight restrictions were removed. The ferry operator, who had enjoyed an estimated annual income of £900, was awarded the sum of £26,557 by way of compensation, since the ferry would no longer be required subsequent to the bridge being built.

The Development of the Railway — Chester–Holyhead

By the 1830s, the Government realised that it was imperative that an improved Irish Mail railway route be established between London and Dublin. With the expansion of the railway network in Britain came the opportunity to establish a direct link. The two routes under consideration were from London to Shrewsbury and then, via Bala, to the coast at Porthdinllaen and from London to Chester and then along the north Wales coast. In the case of the former, W. A. Maddocks, who had developed the town of Tremadoc, saw many advantages in

---

* During the time when the bridge was under construction and the Strait closed to navigation, £100 was distributed among the Menai Strait ship's pilots as compensation for the losses they sustained during the stoppage.

Porthdinllaen being the port for Ireland since it would bring trade, albeit passing, into the area and, in particular, to his town.

Charles Vignoles was asked to carry out a survey of possible alternatives but, since he considered the north Wales coast route as being totally unsuitable from the outset, because of various natural obstacles such as Penmaenbach and Penmaenmawr, he concentrated his efforts on the route ending at Porthdinllaen. Although such a route was not without its problems, he was totally dedicated in presenting his case in opposition to Robert Stephenson, who was asked to survey the north Wales coast route, initially as far as Llandudno (also known as Ormeshead). The possibility of developing Ormeshead as a harbour suitable for Irish mail boats, would have obviated the necessity of building a rail bridge across the Menai Strait. However, this idea was soon abandoned.

Subsequent to surveying Holyhead harbour on behalf of the Admiralty, and its favourable findings, Robert Stephenson undertook the detailed examination of extending the railway line from Chester to Holyhead in 1838, considered the shortest line of communication between London and Dublin, on behalf of the Chester & Crewe Railway Company. Such a survey had to take into consideration, not only the crossing of the Conwy river and the Menai Strait, two very difficult obstacles, but also the arduous undertaking of extending a railway line along the north Wales coastal terrain.

The Britannia Tubular Bridge

The point which Stephenson chose for his rail crossing of the Menai Strait, was where the Britannia Rock could be used to support the central pier and upon which the ends of the tubes would be supported. The choice of design and method of construction was again dictated by a directive from the Admiralty, which specified that any bridge which was to be built for the purpose of carrying the railway from the mainland to Anglesey, would have to be 100 feet above high water.

The Britannia Tubular Bridge, of much larger dimensions than the Conwy Bridge, but designed in a similar manner, started with the building of the tower on the Britannia rock directly in the middle of the Strait in May 1846. This work was undertaken over a period of months, since it could only be carried out at suitable stages of the tide. The eventual height of the tower, including its foundation, reached 230 feet. The work on the towers on either side of the main tower and abutments was carried out in a similar manner.

The four main tubes, each 472 feet in length, were constructed on staging on the Caernarfon side, whilst the

Three views of the Britannia tubular bridge under construction, 1848/9, by G. Hawkins [National Library of Wales]

Maintenance workers inside one of the tubes. [British Rail] smaller tubes leading from the abutments, were built *in situ*. Eight pontoons were used to move the tubes in turn, from the shore to a position where they could be raised on to their resting place within the towers. This was accomplished, by positioning the pontoons beneath the tubes, at low water, in two groups of four. The first tube was floated in June 1849 and formed the Anglesey large span of the up line. The movement of the pontoons was controlled by four capstans, two positioned on both shores, each handled by 50 labourers. All four tubes had been floated by 25 July 1850. Each tube weighed 1800 tons and had to be lifted 100 feet above the pontoon, to its final position within the towers, by means of a hydraulic press. During the lifting of the first tube on 17 August, 1849, and after attaining a height of nearly 20 feet, the bottom of the hydraulic press on the Anglesey tower burst, causing the tube to drop. Fortunately, due to the packing that had been placed underneath, this was only a one inch drop and damage to the tube was avoided (part of this hydraulic cylinder can still be seen near the present Britannia Bridge, as can a section of the tube). The other three tubes were raised without any major problems. The four lions, symbolic guardians of the bridge, are each 25 feet long, 12 feet in height and weigh about 30 tons. They are intended to be in harmony with the original work, as they represent the boldness and strength of the venture (they can now be seen from the roadway beneath the bridge). A colossal figure of Britannia was intended for the centre tower of the bridge, but its cost precluded its construction. The bridge was completed 25 July 1850.

To enable Queen Victoria, Prince Albert and the Prince of Wales to visit the bridge in October 1852, the Royal party left the Penrhyn Arms Hotel in Bangor at 9.30am in carriages and proceeded over the Menai Suspension Bridge to Llanfairpwll station, where they were met by Robert Stephenson. Whilst the Queen travelled through the tube in the State Carriage, drawn by men rather than by an engine, Prince Albert and the Prince of Wales, accompanied by Stephenson, walked on the roof of the tube to the other side.

In order that the tubes would be protected from the weather, they had the benefit of a timber roof covered in tarred hessian. When this caught fire on 23 May 1970 it spread very quickly, initially along one tube then on to the other creating a huge blaze, no doubt intensified by the multi-layers of tar applied over the years. The intense heat soon reduced the tubes to a plastic state, causing both to sag. By the time the fire had burnt itself out and the tubes had cooled, it was found that sagging, which was up to 29 inches in parts, had caused them to split. Urgent remedial work was carried out by the Royal Engineers to prevent a worsening of the situation.

It took ten years to reconstruct the Tubular Bridge with a structure that was not dissimilar in design to that submitted to the Admiralty *c.*1836, but rejected because the overall height was less than 100 feet above high water. The arches for the new Britannia Bridge had to be of sufficient strength to carry, not only the original railway line, but also a roadway on a higher level.

The small tidal harbour at Felinheli, now used as a marina, was taken over for use as a fitting-up ground for the fabricated steelwork for the arches which, when assembled into bays three arch ribs wide, was transferred to pontoons and towed to the bridge. With the pontoons held in position by mooring buoys and anchor points on land, each bay was lifted by gantries which travelled along the top of the tubes. Upon completion of the arches the tubes were removed and the two levels constructed. A monument to the seven men who lost their lives during the construction of the tubular bridge (1846–1850) and the two men who died during the reconstruction (1972–3), can be seen at the nearby church cemetery.

The re-opening of the bridge in 1980 was the catalyst to the building of the A55 dual-carriage roadway, which by now extends from Holyhead to Chester, enabling traffic to travel unhindered, in total contrast to the problems which travellers had previously encountered.

A 1980 artist's impression of the re-constructed Britannia Bridge after the disastrous 1970 fire. [British Rail]

Below: A passenger train emerging from the east portal of the Britannia Bridge, showing the inscription 'Erected Anno Domini MDCCCL, Robert Stephenson, Engineer' and two of the four leonine sentinels; 'Pedwar llew tew, heb ddim blew. Dau'r ochr yma, a dau'r ochor drew.'
[British Rail]

A British Railways locomotive stands in Port Dinorwic station, 1950s. [British Rail]

The Development of the Railway to Caernarfon

In November 1850, an application was submitted by the Chester and Holyhead Railway to Parliament for extending the line from Menai Bridge, where a junction had been constructed, to Caernarfon. Even when granted, it was still necessary to seek the permission of the landowners for the line to pass through their property. The fact that compensation was paid in accordance with the value of the land taken, no doubt assisted the owner to come to a favourable decision. As far as Lord Boston was concerned, compensation was decided at £580, which he accepted rather than 'be drawn to a fussy arbitration'.

The Bangor and Caernarfon Railway Company was incorporated in 1851 and the single line to Port Dinorwic was opened for goods traffic 1 March 1852 and to passengers through to Caernarfon 1 July 1852. However, prior to its opening, discussion had taken place regarding the course of the road through Port Dinorwic. The original toll road, after passing through Bush farm, proceeded through Augusta Street, as it had always done, before joining the 1837 Caernarfon Road. However, the route of the railway would have necessitated the use of a level crossing. A letter dated 21 February 1852 stated, 'The railway company say they intend to open all the way to Caernarvon early in April so that the bridge, cutting, land and all must be made in about six weeks … (and) getting rid of the level crossing'. An approach was made to the trustees of the turnpike road, under the chairmanship of Lord Newborough, for the road to be diverted so that the railway would cross the road by means of a bridge, thus dispensing with a level crossing. Both the Trustees and Lord Boston agreed to this course. Once implemented and the new road completed, Augusta Street became Augusta Place.

Additional land was acquired in 1871, which not only allowed the line through to Caernarfon to be doubled, but also enabled a new station and a siding to be built nearer the developing village.

4. Quay and Harbour

Until the early seventeenth century, those journeying between Bangor and Caernarfon, either on foot or horseback, travelled a lonely road, the few houses that were encountered being mostly concentrated in the hamlet of Aberpwll. It was here that a mill was built, powered by water diverted along the mill-race from the Afon Heilyn. According to a report in *Yr Herald Gymraeg* of 8 October, 1864, Mr Williams of Vaenol decided, in 1633, to build a new mill on the side of the inlet within reach of the sea and located in a position where the maximum benefit would be derived from the tides. Originally called Aber Heilyn, it then became Aber y Felin and eventually Felinheli. Eventually, the silting up of both the river and the inlet caused it to cease operating. The newspaper report stated that the last miller was William Gray and that by *c.*1783 the building had fallen into disuse as a mill but, much to the consternation of the local people who apparently deplored such activity, the site had thereafter been used for cock-fighting, a popular sport in the late eighteenth century.

The demise of the mill coincided with the period when slates intended for export were being transported in increasing quantities from Dinorwic Quarry down to the coast. The following figures give an indication of the quantities involved and their prices (the descriptive names given to the slates and which were attributed to a General Warburton *c.*1765, merely indicate their sizes):

> Account of slate sold out of Thomas Assheton Smith Quarries in Dinorwick [sic] in the county of Carnarvon from 30.10.1787 to 22.8.1788 inclusive:
>
> | | |
> |---|---|
> | 71,000 Countesses at 2/2d per thousand | £309 2/- |
> | 151,750 Ladies at 1/1d per thousand | £159 6. 9d. |
> | 25,000 Doubles at 11d per thousand | £ 68 15/- |
> | 456 tons 10 cwt of slate at 1/2d per ton | £502 2/- |
> | Charges in connection with the above: | |
> | raising 171,000 Countesses @ 16/- | £136 |
> | carriage   *do*   *do*   @ 14/- | £119 |

[PYA 29097-8]

However, although the quantity of slate being exported was increasing, it appears — according to an observation made by Assheton Smith's agent in 1789 — that the record of slate being handled was anything but accurate:

> For want of correct and regular accounts of all the slates which have been delivered both at Moel y Don and Carnarvon many mistakes have been made … which cannot be rectified. It would therefore be necessary to procure an authority from the Customs House of all vessels cleared out with Mr T. A. Smith's slate.   [PYA 29106]

In the latter part of the eighteenth and early nineteenth centuries, the Customs House referred to above described as a '… small and mean building (but) conveniently situated …', stood against the castle walls, near to the Anglesey Arms.

The type of incidental costs involved with the loading of slate during this period were:

1787 Paid for ale allowed in loading *Mary J. Owen* 2/- '(PYA 29100) … Thomas Jones 24 June 1790 piling slate at Moel y Don and Carnarvon £1 1/- … loading vessel *Industry* (commanded by Capt. Lewis Evans): 41,500 Countesses, 22,000 ladies, 10,000 doubles and Straw to put between the piles £1 1/- [PYA 29114-5].

The new road built in 1812 down Nant y Garth provided, what was considered at the time, an expeditious method of carrying slate from Fachwen to Aberpwll, but even the introduction of horse-drawn carts rather than the hitherto use of mules, could not keep pace with the increasing demand for slate. Consequently, this method was supplemented in 1824 with the construction of a tramway built more or less parallel with the road. These horse-drawn wagons, having delivered slates to the wharf, would return to the quarry laden with goods for the quarry such as '… planks, a cask or two of blasting powder, 3–400 pieces of iron …'.

Although the wharfs that were built near the old mill, including those for which Thomas Assheton Smith was responsible in 1793 [DQ 3464], allowed small sailing vessels to be loaded with slate, lightering continued to be the method of loading larger vessels at anchor on the Strait. In 1802, three additional berths were built within the inlet at Aberpwll, between the point where the old mill was located and the present bridge which crosses from one side of the harbour to the other. Further improvements continued to be made in the first half of the 19th century to cope with increasing trade, by extending from the old sea wall towards the upper part of the inlet. However, this was still a tidal basin thus restricting both the movement of ships and the size that could be accommodated.

During the period between 1820–45, when slate was being exported to America, payment documents referred to the point of loading as Moel y Don, even though earlier in the 19th century it was being referred to as Velin Heli [*North Wales Gazette* 20.3.1817]. The *Favourite* from New York, with Thomas Fanning as master, was one such vessel taking 150,000 large Ladies (£300) and 100,000 small Ladies (£125) on March 24 1821. The brigantine *Horizon* was another, which came from New York under Captain Thomas Clark on April 15 1823 taking 20,000 Countesses, 40,000 large Ladies, 88,000 small Ladies and 96,000 Doubles. The vessel *William* of Portsmouth, New Hampshire, USA, under the command of Captain Charles Harris, which sailed from Velinheli on June 1 1824 for New York loaded with 25,000 Countesses, and 2,000 Ladies with a total value of £458 3s. 9d., would no doubt have been lightered at Moel y Don. This method would also have applied in August 1824 when the *America*, also of Portsmouth, New Hampshire, USA, under the command of Captain Samuel Pray, was being loaded with 144,000 Ladies, 44,000 small Ladies costing £360 2s. 6d. for Hugh Matthie & Son of New York. The payment for slates sold by

Harbour pre-1900 with Harbour Master's office on the left. [Author]

Schooners in the old tidal harbour c.1890 with the Elizabeth Bennett *on the extreme right.* [Emyr Wyn Roberts]

Assheton Smith was handled by his bankers, Williams & Company at Caernarfon

Sir Llewelyn Turner of Parkia, Caernarfon stated that his father, William Turner, who managed slate quarries and copper mines on behalf of Assheton Smith in the early part of the nineteenth century, recalled the many vessels involved in the export of slate to many parts of the world from Port Dinorwic. Over the years, William Turner came to know many of the men who commanded these vessels and one captain in particular, aware that it would be his last visit to the port, offered his father any item off the ship as a gift. He chose a blunderbuss, an item which he had always admired when visiting the vessel. All merchant ships carried some means of defence, usually in the form of cannons in the latter part of the eighteenth and beginning of the nineteenth centuries, against marauding well-armed privateer vessels. Llewelyn Turner recalls seeing one such vessel, the *Endeavour*, tied up alongside a yard (later de Winton's foundry) in Caernarfon c.1850.

Loading slate on to the SS Vaynol *at the old dock (Cei Mawr), 1896. The estate yard can be seen in the background.* [Gwynedd Archives Service]

When the second Thomas Assheton Smith (1776–1858) inherited the Vaynol estate in 1828, he decided to change the name of the village from Felinheli to Port Dinorwic, because of its slate quarrying connection. It was also the time when there was an increasing use being made of new wharfs built within the inlet, which allowed vessels, albeit of small tonnage, to be loaded directly from the shore rather than by lightering. A 'New Quay', built between 23 November 1839 and 12 January 1841, facilitated not only the storage and dispatch of slate from Port Dinorwic, it also allowed larger ships to tie-up alongside [PYA 29092].

Twenty-five years later, further improvements to the old harbour were considered necessary, as indicated in a letter sent by Millington, agent for Vaynol, to C. Cecil Trevor of the Board of Trade, Whitehall on May 3 1867:

> In accordance with your letter of the 3rd ult. I beg to enclose herewith for the approval of the Board, Duplicate Plan and Section of the Quay proposed to be made (in pursuance of their covenant) by the Trustees of George Wm. Duff Assheton Smith Esq. on a portion of the Foreshore of the Menai Straits lying between Port Dinorwic and Dinas, leased to them from the Crown … . [GAS, VP 2379].

With an increasing number of ships arriving at Felinheli to be loaded with slate, a method had to be devised as to the order of loading. The captains would meet at 11am each morning, outside the quay office, which stood below Port Terrace, where a board was displayed indicating the cargo to be loaded and its destination. They would then decide amongst themselves which ship would take a particular cargo. Another factor, which should have been taken into consideration when applying cargoes to certain ships, was the question as to the order in which they should be loaded but, according to a report that appeared in the *Caernarfon & Denbigh Herald* on February 5 1870, it was not carried out in an equitable manner:

> We have many times been appealed to, to expose the injury done to the owners of local vessels plying between Port Dinorwic and the various places to which the Slate Quarries send their produce. But after the expose two years ago of a similar abuse of power (at Bangor) we had hoped that it would not have been necessary to return to the subject … the injustice which we … believe was honourably redressed, still exists at Port Dinorwic … . We would ask the ship owners generally who go to Port Dinorwic for cargoes, expecting to be loaded in rotation, are they satisfied that they do get their turn honestly? If they do not, why not at once appeal to the principal? If he acquiesces in the course pursued then let them decide for themselves whether it is desirable to go to Port Dinorwic at all. Our aim is to redress a supposed wrong. If the parties interested are satisfied with the course pursued, then we have nothing more to say. But if they are, it is hard to understand the denunciations uttered against certain individuals interested in the ownership of the above named vessels (a list of ships was shown with the names of the purported owners or individuals with an interest). It is no doubt true that a great many of these vessels trade beyond seas, and do not effect local trade; but it only shows the extent to which the local quarry agents are interested in shipping … .

Similar comments and complaints were being expressed by a ship's captain:

> 22 July 1883 — We are here yet; they have promised to load me every day. We are first on turn. This last three weeks not one vessel has been loaded of our size. I am ashamed to be here so long but I cannot help it. They told me this morning that we are sure to be loaded shortly … .
>
> 1 August 1883 — We are very near loaded for Port Glasgow in the Clyde. I am afraid we wont be loaded today on account of no slate down. We want only about 5 tons to complete. Freight: 10/6 a ton. I have no nus (sic) to tell … .

The New Harbour

As the turn of the century was nearing and with an ever increasing demand for slate, G. W. D. Assheton Smith decided to rebuild the harbour at Port Dinorwic, so as to facilitate the loading and unloading of ships within a lock-gate system. On 10 April 1897, an agreement was signed between Philip Ayres of Ayres and Company and Assheton Smith for its construction. This, the largest undertaking for the port with lock gates being built by Cleghorn and Wilkinson, Engineers, Northwich, cost £18,527. When work started on the 26 March 1897, Afon

Reconstruction of the harbour with the Afon Heilyn contained within a wooden trough. [Gwynedd Archives Service]

Reconstruction of the harbour, 1897–1900. [Gwynedd Archives Service]

General view of the quay and dock, c.1937. [Author]

Heilyn, which normally flowed into the inlet, was contained within a wooden trough built on the Bangor side of the eventual harbour, thus enabling it to flow to the open sea without inhibiting work on the harbour.

Many conditions were incorporated into the 1897 contract including:

… contractor to erect and maintain … a temporary bridge of timber or other material across the entrance of the big lock by the pier head. One portion of the bridge not exceeding 30 feet may be fixed but the remainder about 40 feet must be capable of opening readily, the operation not requiring more than three minutes to allow vessels to pass in and out. The bridge … must be sufficiently substantial to bear safely the moving load of a train of slate trucks in the roughest weather … [GAS, VP 2764]

[The contractor must ask] … for permission to close the entrance to the works against the incoming tide by a temporary dam … temporary footbridge 2 feet wide erected while the swing bridge is removed and broken up excepting the handrails…which must be carefully removed without injury…existing gas and water pipes and telephone cable … relaid in a trench in the new dock …

The contract provides for the entire completion…in the event of non completion by that date for the payment of a fine or penalty by the Contractor of £10 per day until the works are complete and handed over and also for a premium or bonus of £50 to be paid by the Proprietor for each full week in the event of the work being completed and handed over one week or more earlier than the Contractor date …

The new harbour was opened on 10 September 1900 [DQ 2763, VP 2379]. The first ship to be loaded after the opening was (no doubt by arrangement) the SS *Vaynol* [XM 5583].

An interesting aspect which was under discussion then, and subsequently, was the question of the site of the old mill. This arose shortly after the alterations to the harbour had been completed, since it was relevant to the high water mark and Crown boundary. A letter from Carter Vincent & Co., 4 Church Street, Caernarfon 12 November 1903 to Hasties, London stated:

Before employing anyone to discover the site of the old mill it occurred to me that it would be a wise thing to have the quarry engineer down from Llanberis and see what he would make of the question. I gave him the old entrance plans and instructed him to prove from these the site of the old mill and he located the site of the old mill close to the inner gate of the lock. On comparing this with Oswell's (the engineer who built the dock) plan it coincides with where that gentleman records having found the old foundations of the mill and also with where the mill is shewn by Mr Fred Jackson's other Vaynol Estate plans. In face of these facts Mr Vivian and myself think that it is hardly necessary to employ any other surveyor unless you and Mr Danckwort are still of opinion that it would be advisable … . [DQ 2765-6-7, 2778]

Contemporary maps appear to confirm that, when the mill was working, it stood on the Bangor side of the dock near the inside lock, but at a lower level compared to the present dock side level [XDQ 2777].

Later correspondence stated:

Mr Danckwort thought … the site of the Old Mill was on the brink of the Straits … .

When Ernest Neele, agent to Vaynol Estate, wrote to Hasties 16 November 1903 he made the observation:

… the quarry engineer … located the site of the Mill close to the inner gate of the lock … (and this) coincided with where … (Oswell, engineer) found the old foundations of the Mill … .

Quay Workers

When the village was still in the early stages of development at the start of the nineteenth century, the number of people available to work on the quay were but few, consequently even wives assisted in the loading of the slate on to the ships at a rate of 1/- per day.

The handling of slate generally was a hard and difficult task, even into the twentieth century. When the weather was bad, especially during the winter months, the only additional protection was a sack draped over the shoulders which would be replaced with another when saturated. As a form of protection against the sharp edges of slate, pieces of rubber would be tied to the hands and round the waist as a form of apron.

Work was allocated between eight gangs of loaders, with three in each gang, as this was regarded as the optimum number but, if there were a number of ships waiting to be loaded, then additional workers would be employed on a day-to-day basis so as to clear any back-log.

The teams, made up of a stevedore and two assistants, used special flat-bottomed barrows to move the stored slate, either for loading on to a railway truck or on to a ship. Although Assheton Smith had a reputation for fairness with his employees at a time when unions had not yet been established, wages paid to those who worked on the quay were low compared to workers in other ports. Since the quay workers were paid according to the weight handled ($1/7^{1}/_4$ per ton), wages varied considerably, depending, not only on the size of slate being handled, but also the vehicle being loaded, since a railway truck could be loaded much quicker than a ship. Consequently, it was the normal practice for the gangs to be moved once a month, so that everyone had a change of job and location and the opportunity of equitable earnings.

This altruistic attitude applied also to the casual workers or *hobliwr* as they were called, who presented themselves for work at the quay office each workday. On arrival, their names would be taken and work would be allocated strictly in accordance with the list, without favouritism. For those over the age of 70 and still having to work for the sake of some income, they were allocated lighter duties, such as keeping the place safe and tidy, with bits and pieces of slate raked and collected in a specially adapted wagon.

The larger quarry ships, with their deeper holds, needed teams of five loaders compared to the normal team of three used for the smaller ships, such as the *Velinheli*. A pile of slates, which varied in number depending on their size and thickness, would be placed on a plank by the man on the quay and these would slide down to the man positioned on the deck of the ship, who would control both the speed and direction of the pile on their way to the hold, where the third man awaited them. The remaining two members of the team were responsible for the

stacking within the hold and ensuring that they were properly stowed against possible damage during the voyage.

Just prior to the Second World War, there were 130 men working regularly on the quay and, although Welsh was the normal day-to-day language, many English words were in use such as 'trucks' referring to the main-line as compared to 'wagons' which worked on narrow-gauge in the quarry and on the quay. Other English words heard were 'engine' and 'incline' together with the dimension of the slates.

With the arrival of the four loaded wagons at the bottom of the Penscoins incline, they were unhitched from the wire rope and safety chains and pushed a few feet to the nearby weighing platform. If the wagons were too well oiled, they could be stopped by inserting a steel rod in a purpose built hole in the wheel and held until the wagon was ready to be dealt with. In the 1930s, between 1,500 and 1,800 tons of slate arrived from the quarry per week and were weighed and counted in groups of three, with the Welsh word '*mwrw*' used for such a group. After counting 42 slates or 14 groups of three, they were marked with a steel pin by the counting official and odd numbers over the figure of 42 being marked separately. Usually a certain type and size of slate would be confined to its own wagon but, if there were insufficient number to fill a void, other sizes would be used. The number and type, or quality, of slate was always chalked on the wagon, together with the loader's initials and point of origin of the slate in the quarry.

The office clerk was responsible for recording, in a large ledger, not only the weight of the wagon but, also, other details as given to him by the counters outside, which would include the number of slates, type, point of origin and loader's initial. Similar records were kept at the quarry, allowing a reconciliation to be made and, if a discrepancy arose, this would be investigated by the general manager.

The weighing machine, made by H. Pulley & Son and capable of weighing up to six tons, had to be adjusted daily since its accuracy was affected by the weather. This adjustment was made by adding water to a tank until a pointer indicated a 'normal' position. Further tests for accuracy were conducted every two months by the weighing machine makers and a certificate to this effect was kept in the office.

The wagons, hauled, towards the end of the nineteenth century, by the small narrow gauge steam locomotives and, later, by diesel locomotives, were taken for unloading on to the quayside, with sizes up to 18"x10" stored between the bridge and the dry-dock and larger sizes stored on the sea side of the bridge, hence the reason for marshalling together all the wagons carrying the same size of slate.

Port Dinorwic dry-dock technicians worked closely with their counterparts at the Dinorwic Quarry workshops at Gilfach Ddu, Llanberis and this reciprocal arrangement, with expertise and facilities being shared, worked extremely well over many years. Repairs were not confined to ships belonging to the Dinorwic Quarry Co. Any vessel, provided it did not exceed approximately 180 feet in length, could be accommodated in the dry-dock. According to the 1911 records kept by E. E. Neele, Coppack's ships from Connah's Quay for example, were regularly surveyed and overhauled there. Other ships mentioned were the SS *Lincolnshire*, which had extensive repairs carried out to the engine room and the SS *Briton*, which had a new funnel fitted. Invariably, whilst a ship was in dry-dock, the opportunity would be taken to check and clean the hull and, if necessary, give it a fresh coat of paint, as was the case with the 145 foot SS *Bangor*, belonging to the Anglesey Shipping Co., which required 'two coats of black varnish amounting to 27 gallons and 'boot-topping' requiring 65lbs for the first coat and 53 lbs for the second'.

The 1920 notebook stated that the SS *Penrhyn* had a new 'scotch' boiler measuring 13' x 10', with three furnaces and smoke-box fitted at a cost of £2,830, and she was followed shortly afterwards by the old steamer *Panmure* having a new propeller fitted. As far as the ship's crew were concerned, dry-docking a ship was not popular, as it meant a cut in pay or even being signed off for the duration of the repairs.

London & North Western Railway

When the line between Chester and Holyhead was completed, a branch line was built, initially to Felinheli by the contractors McCormick & Holmes with the first train arriving in March 1852. Shortly after the line was extended from Port Sidings junction to the quay.

Where sections of the narrow gauge rail passed over the mainline rails down on the quay, these were removed at midday to allow the London and North Western Railway engine to bring empty trucks and collect loaded ones via the junction at Port Sidings. The rails were then replaced at 1pm, in time for renewal of work by the narrow gauge locomotives and wagons. The man responsible for the daily ritual with the rails was paid an extra 5/- per month on top of his normal wage. The empty trucks were left on the sloping approach to the quay, enabling them to be positioned where and when required by a man riding on the back of the truck, with his foot controlling the brake.

With the arrival of the railway at Felinheli, more and more slates were being transported by this method as compared to the hitherto use of ships, especially since the railway system was not affected by the vagaries of the weather and was able to deliver promptly with fewer breakages. It also eliminated much of the loading and unloading, which was inevitable when transport was by ship and was able to

Transferring slate from quarry wagons to mainline railway wagons, c.1950. [Author]

cope with smaller quantities of slate when so required. With so much competition between the two systems, inevitably the cost of freight was reduced in both cases, more especially since the railway system at that time was able to deliver between town and town, whereas the ships relied on delivery to ports, with onward transport of the slate to its ultimate destination by whatever means available. With the disposal of the Dinorwic Quarry ships during the 1950s, and the closing of the Padarn railway, it became easier and more economical for slates to be transported by road from the quarry directly to the site where they were required.

5. Sea Cadets and Master Mariners

Until the early part of the nineteenth century, youngsters in north west Wales, who were keen on a career at sea, usually spent the early years on board a ship working as cook and bottle washer and learning through experience. To qualify as an able-seaman, and thereby gain an increase in wage, it was necessary to be well-versed in such matters as carpentry (even though the ship carried a carpenter), sail repairing and being able to handle and store cargo.

Not all of the youngsters were sufficiently ambitious to want to become master mariners, but those who did, until the law decreed otherwise, had 'to pass the club', which meant undergoing an examination by the 'directors of the club', composed of master mariners who had spent many years experiencing every situation which a sailor could expect during a lifetime at sea. Success in such an oral examination was usually followed by a great deal of friendly advice. With the introduction of the Merchant Shipping Acts of 1851 and 1854 [GAS XM4558/57], all masters were compelled to have a Board of Trade Certificate of Proficiency. However, those who had been in command for a specific period prior to 1854, were not required to sit the Board of Trade examination.

Local Tuition

It appears from a letter dated 3 March 1815 from Richard Garnons, c/o Marine & Commercial School of Carnarvon, to Lord Anglesey, that there was a need to establish a maritime school in the town and, at the same time, both improve the Castle Square or Green as it was then called, and use the spoil from such work to improve the harbour:

> I have had the honour of laying your Lordship's letter of the 14th of Feby. before a meeting of the subscribers to the Carnarvon Marine & Commercial School & I am requested by them to express the high sense they entertain of your Lordship's kindness in Patronizing the School ... I have inclosed a rough sketch ... of the spot, on which it is proposed to erect the school & ... a Plan has been suggested to the Trustees of the Harbour, to lower about 5 feet of the surface of the Castle Green, which would bring it upon a level with the road from the Goat Inn to Nelson Street & to carry that soil down to assist in filling up the New Quay and to continue a road from the Bridge across the Castle Green down to the New Quay — should this Plan be executed at any future period the school house would stand upon a terrace above the intended road ... .   [UCNW-PN 2058]

Another account which appears to confirm that it was the intention of the town dignitaries to improve and extend the quay stated:

> ... the huge mound of earth was removed about the year 1817 ... (the corporation) employed the poor ... in removing the earth and wheeling it down to improve the quay, which had been erected c.1803 — has lately been extended. The quay wall had been built against piles and the rubbish taken from the green thrown behind and levelled ... . The Castle Hotel was built in 1834 and the Post Office opened in the square in 1880 ... .

William Jones, a Pwllheli shipbuilder, made this observation about the state of education and, in particular, how it affected his trade:

> I often want Masters and Mates for [a] great number of ships but I can find none in this place. It is necessary to go elsewhere to find them; it is so in my shipyard; it is so amongst the trades people. The young men of twenty years of age have not been taught and consequently they cannot even make out a bill. Very few indeed can read English; but they are able to read the Bible in Welsh but they can do no more … .

Youngsters living in or near Caernarfon intending to enter for the Board of Trade examinations and wishing to make the sea their career had, according to the Town Directory of 1886, the benefit of a 'Teacher of Navigation', Ellen Edwards of 13 Tithebarn Street, Caernarfon. She was the widow of Owen Edwards and had, according to her gravestone at Llanbeblig churchyard and her obituary [*C&DH*, 29 November 1889], taught navigation in Caernarfon for 60 years. Although available records do not support the theory, it may well be that she had been schooled in the subject by her father, Captain William Francis, who had retired from the sea so as to run a 'Commercial, Classical and Mathematical Instruction at Amlwch' [advert, *North Wales Gazette*, 6 January 1825]. Although the 1847 Education Commission report for Llanbeblig (Caernarfon) wrote in derogatory terms of the local teaching facilities, it is unlikely that the term 'old woman' referred to Ellen Edwards, since she would only have been about 37 years of age at the time, if the dates given in the newspaper reporting her death are correct.

> There has been no education whatever for the sailors of this port. They know nothing of navigation except a sort of knack which they have acquired by practice and by tradition. All the navigation which has been learned here as a science has been taught by an old woman of Carnarvon. This is not confined to the port of Carnarvon; it is generally the case throughout the country … .

When she died, a local newspaper [*C&DH*, 29 November, 1889] stated:

DEATH OF A REMARKABLE OLD LADY AT CARNARVON
… hundreds of Welsh seamen heard with deep regret of the death at the age of 79 after a prolonged illness of Mrs Edwards the very notable and successful teacher of navigation for nearly sixty years. Mrs Ellen Edwards, who was a native of Amlwch, was known far and wide as the most successful seamen's teacher in North Wales … . Her funeral was a remarkable one as the cortege consisted of a large number of master mariners, mates, seamen and nearly all the naval reserve not on duty in the town … .

It also stated that '… in 1881, through the good offices of Sir Llewelyn Turner, the deceased lady received a grant of £75 out of the Royal Bounty Fund in recognition of her long and meritorious services...'.

Youngsters who were not in a position to receive formal training but who were, nevertheless, keen on a career at sea, would resort to private tuition in navigation supplemented by actual experience on board ship.

Although unqualified, Thomas Ellis Hughes of Glandon, Beach Road, Port Dinorwic, having the technical knowledge and sea-going experience, was capable of teaching his pupils navigation to the standard required for them to sit their examinations at Liverpool. Amongst the variety of topics that Thomas Griffiths (1781–1861) taught at his 'one penny a week' school at Siloh, Felinheli, was navigation for the benefit of the many youngsters who wished to make the sea their careers. Hugh Davies, who kept a navigation school at Pen y Graig, Nevin, was similarly qualified to provide tuition based on experience [UCNW-BC 11837]. In 1910, Bottwnog Grammar School on the Lleyn peninsular, an area which had produced a great many master mariners over the years, appointed a master to teach navigation and mathematics to those pupils keen to make the sea their career.

Clio Training Ship

When Charles Kingsley, Canon Residentiary of Chester Cathedral, established an industrial training school in 1875 for 'homeless, destitute and poor respectable boys sent in by magistrates' he was given the choice of two ships by the Admiralty: the *St. George* and the *Clio*. It was decided that the *Clio*, a three-masted, sixteen gun corvette, 211' long and 33' 7" wide, would be the most suitable. She had been built of African oak with beams of mahogany at Sheerness in 1860 [UCNW, BC 34582]. Anchored in 1877 about 300 yards to the north-west of the Bangor pier-head, she was used to train from 250–300 'Homeless, Destitute, unconvicted and Poor Respectable Boys' of between 11 and 16 years of age from North Wales, City of Chester and border counties for the Merchant Service and Navy'. There were many conditions and tests before a boy could be accepted for training and he had to be of sound constitution, free from mental or physical defect and a potential sailor. Although one condition of entry stated that children had to be free from criminal convictions, children of 12 years of age and upwards could be sent to the *Clio* if '... brought before two justices or magistrate if ... found begging or receiving alms ... wandering and not having

Annual Report of the Clio, *1879. [Author]*

Trainees parade aboard the Clio *complete with band. [Author]*

any home … destitute due to being an orphan or having a parent in prison … frequents the company of reputed thieves …' There were also cases where parents or guardians were anxious to place children under naval discipline, as it was felt that '… their energies, properly directed, often turn out the best sailors' [GAS XM 2333].

A proportion of the boys were supported financially but others, because of poverty or parental neglect, were educated, fed and clothed free of charge. The cost of running the ship was £5,311 per annum, with the Treasury providing £3,161 and the remainder being provided from private sources. Of the total sum spent on running the ship, £20 was spent annually in feeding, clothing and educating each boy.

Parents or other relatives were allowed to correspond with the boys at 'reasonable times', but all letters to or from the boys were opened by the Captain for checking. They were allowed to visit them only once in two months, on an appointed day, but this could be disallowed if the boy misbehaved. An application had to be made to the Captain and Superintendent who would issue a ticket indicating the time of the visit. No one was allowed on board during the week without the consent of the Captain, and visitors on Sunday were confined to members of the public who were invited to attend the evening church service — 'Visitors may signal the ship from the pier for a boat to convey them to the ship and back for a trifling fee …'. The *Clio* brass and bugle bands would often entertain visitors to the ship and also during regattas on shore.

The *Clio* was run by the Captain and Superintendent, together with 13 officers and the school was divided into five classes I, II, III, IV, V with 63, 80, 59, 37 and 20 boys respectively in each class. A strong element of competition was generated amongst the boys and prizes were awarded annually in seamanship, carpentry, sailmaking, tailoring, shoemaking, cookery, laundry, barber, best singer, most popular boy, best at gun drill, rifle drill and cutlass drill also for the best petty officer. In addition to such a range of subjects, the boys were also instructed in writing, reading and arithmetic. At the time of the 1883 award ceremony there were 237 boys on board the *Clio* [*NWC*, 14.7.1883].

Any punishment applied for bad behaviour had to be recorded, together with the nature of the offence. Punishment could take the form of forfeiture of rewards and privileges, reduction in quality and quantity of food, confinement in a room or lighted cell for not more than three days, or moderate personal correction not exceeding twelve strokes with a birch or cane. No child was to be deprived of two meals in succession and any boy in confinement was allowed not less than 1lb of bread and gruel daily.

A report, published in 1879, stated that the health of the boys was very good, but there were several cases of frostbite during severe weather and one boy had lost some of his toes. Some deaths did occur amongst the boys on board the

Some of the youngsters who died on board the Clio *are buried in Llandegfan. [Author]*

Clio either through accident or illness. Seven boys died between 1875, when the *Clio* was established, and 1883 [*NWC*, 14.7.1883]. William Crook, who died on 5 January, 1905, was taken, as was the custom, on a gun carriage pulled by the boys up Gazelle hill, along the main road and then up Cechla hill, with the band in attendance, to Llandegfan church where he was buried.

When the time came for the boys, who had survived the strict regime, to leave the *Clio* at the age of 16, many would go to sea, although they had the choice of returning home if they so wished [*C&DH*, 17.2.1883 & 5.12.1883]. The *Clio* ceased training May 1919.

HMS *Conway*

In order that youngsters be given the opportunity to train for service in the Merchant Navy, the Mercantile Marine Service Association of Liverpool, formed in 1857, accepted the offer by the Admiralty of the frigate *Conway*, a vessel of 652 tons, to be used as a training ship. Launched at Chatham in 1832 as a 26-gun man-of-war, she had served in the West Indies, the Pacific, China and the Cape Stations for over 20 years before being used as a coastguard at Devonport. It was reported in the *Liverpool Mercury*, on 19 May 1859, that Captain Charles Powell had been appointed commander of this first training-ship. As a result of a report to the Admiralty, endorsed by Lord Clarence Paget, stating that the ship could only accommodate 150 boys and room for training was insufficient, she was replaced by HMS *Winchester*, a 487 ton 60-gun frigate which had been launched in 1816. She was renamed *Conway* but, once again, due to an increasing number of cadets wishing to join the Merchant Navy, the accommodation proved inadequate and unsuitable.

The third and final training ship, a 92-gun battleship of 2,626 tons, had been launched as HMS *Nile* in 1827. Converted to screw in 1852, she was commissioned during the Russian war and served in the Baltic Fleet in 1854 and 1855, before being decommissioned two years later. She was towed from Devonport by the *Valorous*, a paddle-frigate, arriving at Rock Ferry in June 1876. In accordance with tradition, she too was renamed *Conway*.

After a period of over 60 years on the Mersey and subsequent to a close encounter with magnetic mines during the Second World War, the *Conway* was moved to the Menai Strait in May 1941 and moored close to Bangor pier, where the *Clio* training ship had been until 1917. The Conway's captain, Commander T. M. Goddard, whilst writing to Captain Rees Thomas, the harbour-master at Caernarfon, on another matter stated:

> We have settled down in this delightful spot and I can see that I for one will never want to return to the Mersey. A perfect spot one dreams of at sea.

She remained there until 1949 when she was taken to new moorings near Plas Newydd, the home of the Marquess of Anglesey. Although the distance involved was but short, it entailed negotiating the Swellies, a narrow passage which, because of her 22' draft and 54' beam, only allowed 15' on either side of the ship. Since she had the benefit of a spring tide travelling in the same direction, the role of the tugs on that occasion was to ensure that she was kept in the correct channel. Nevertheless, it was the skill of the Menai Strait pilots that brought her safely to Plas Newydd.

When, in 1953, it became necessary for the *Conway* to be taken to Birkenhead for work on her hull, the voyage was to be anything but straightforward. It was decided that the operation had to be carried out in April so as to have the benefit of the spring tides. The *Dongarth* and the *Minegarth*, the same two tugs which had been used four years previously, were again involved.

Left: Conway training ship being brought from Bangor to Plas Newydd by the tugs Dongarth and Minegarth in 1949. [Emyr Wyn Roberts]

Below: Conway being towed from Plas Newydd with the intention of being taken to Birkenhead for repairs but difficulties were experienced because of the strength of the tide. [Ronald Norman]

Below: Menai Strait pilots, R. J. Jones and J. R. Jones on the occasion of the presentation of a cup (13 April 1949) to commemorate the successful transfer of the Conway from Bangor pier to Plas Newydd. [Katie Limerick Jones]

Above: One of the four anchors that held the Conway in position at Plas Newydd now to be seen outside the Caernarfon Maritime Museum on Victoria Dock. [Author]

Left: Conway aground and broken, 1953 [Nancy Tildsley]

Since the timing was critical to the state of the tide, it was imperative that they passed through the Swellies before the westbound tide built up strength. It was also necessary to take into consideration the weather. As it happened, on the day when she was being moved, there was a light to moderate north-westerly breeze blowing which would affect the timing of the slack-water and strength of the tide.

Although the two Menai Strait pilots, Richard John Jones and his son, John Richard Jones, piloted several ships a week through the Swellies and had 40 years' experience between them in such work, the first meeting to which they were invited to discuss the operation was on 30 March 1953. It was at that meeting that R. J. Jones suggested that an extra tug be on hand in case of unforeseen problems, particularly since the *Conway* was a dead ship without engine power or steering gear, but this suggestion was rejected. The only other meeting to which the pilots were invited was on Monday, 13 April, the day before the operation.

On the day of the move, R. J. Jones was aboard the *Conway* and J. R. Jones aboard the tug *Dongarth,* which had the task of towing the *Conway* whilst the *Minegarth* was made-fast aft. Although R. J. Jones had recommended to Captain Hewitt, who was in charge of the operation, that an earlier start be made because of the weather conditions, Captain Hewitt decided not to change his programme.   After passing safely over the Cheese Rock, J. R. Jones was aware that, due to the increasing strength of the tide, less and less progress was being made. He suggested to Captain Hewitt that they should take the ship back by reversing the role of the tugs, but this was not accepted. This suggestion was again repeated when they were passing the Swelly Rock and the tide was running at almost 2 knots, but to no avail. When it was realised that she was no longer making any headway against the tide, the order was given for the *Minegarth* to go ahead and assist the *Dongarth*. This resulted in some headway being made but, due to the strength of the tide and the eddies, she passed over the Platters and went ashore. All attempts at hauling her off failed.

There followed a number of meetings at which the question of ownership of the vessel and subsequent wreck was discussed. Amongst those attending a meeting, held at the Admiralty at 3pm on the 18 August 1954 and representing the Caernarvon Harbour Trust, were Lt. Colonel R. D. Briercliffe, CBE, JP and Captain T. Rees Thomas, Clerk and Superintendent. It was pointed out that the Harbour Trust would not be financially capable of dealing with the wreck, as its income was confined to rent from reclaimed land and from an oil depôt. In an attempt at expediting the disposal of the wreck, the point was made that if the *Conway* broke up it could cause problems with the R.A.S.C. craft based at Beaumaris, the seaplane factory at Beaumaris and the numerous small craft using the Strait. Due to shifting sands, 95% of Caernarfon traffic used the Swellies passage rather than the Caernarfon entrance. The stark report of a survey carried out on the wreck in June 1954, and stating that the after part of the vessel could break away due to a gale or adverse tides, may have expedited its removal.

A contract was signed 30 July 1956 with Underwater Welders and Repairers Ltd., Cardiff for the complete removal of the *Conway* wreck at a cost of £47,200. While the work was being carried out, a fire occurred which burnt out the hull to the level of the orlop deck. Since the fire had reduced the amount of work necessary to clear the wreck, it was argued that the agreed quotation for disposal was unjustified. Nevertheless, counsel's opinion was that the whole sum of £47,200 was still payable, since the salvagers had lost the benefit of salvaging material from the ship. The stage payments that would have been paid to the contractor had the fire not occurred were: clearing to the level of the main deck £7,080; to the level of the upper 'tween deck £7,080; to the level of the lower tween deck £7,080; removal of the hull to the level of the orlop deck £7,080; completion of the removal of the wreck £18,880 [GAS XD15 24/35 – 24/37 Opinion of Counsel re. *Conway* wreck 2.5.1955].

It was a very sad end to a noble vessel which had been responsible for the training of a great many officers for the Merchant Navy over the years.

Master Mariners

Such were the numbers of captains living in Caernarfonshire and Anglesey during the first half of the twentieth century that, when a reunion of Master Mariners was organised on 11 August 1935, at Glynllifon outside Caernarfon, 370 were invited and 170 actually attended. The cost of the reunion was 10/- (50p) per head which covered the cost of hiring a coach, supper, gratuities, fees for the hall, lecture, singer and accompanist. A photograph, taken by Mr Pound, who had a studio in Castle Square, Caernarfon, of those who attended from Port Dinorwic included: Captain W. Jones, Bronfa; Captain R. O. Jones; Captain J. Jones; Captain David Roberts; Captain T. Roberts; Captain Joe Tyldesley; Captain Ben Williams and Captain W. Williams [UCNW, 11547].

Fortunately, three of the master mariners, Captain David Roberts, Captain T. Wilson Roberts and Captain Ben Williams, kept an account of their careers, the latter two with details of actual voyages. It is from these accounts that the following details have been extracted, to serve as an example of the many problems encountered by those who served in sailing ships and learnt their craft 'the hard way' (please see Appendix 1 for details of Felinheli mariners).

Captain David Roberts

Captain Roberts, who was born at his grandparents home at Bryn Hyfryd, Port Dinorwic, started his career at sea with his uncle at the age of twelve, voyaging mostly across the Irish Sea. His family had maritime connections with Bangor and, in particular, with the shipbuilding and repairing yards at Hirael where there were five yards, including the Patent Slip yard at the Garth end, run by Captain J. Ellis, Captain J. Thomas, Henry Owens and

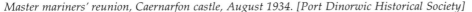

Master mariners' reunion, Caernarfon castle, August 1934. [Port Dinorwic Historical Society]

Owen Roberts. Captain David Roberts recalls on his visits to Port Penrhyn that it was not unusual to see some seventy anchored sailing vessels on the Strait, loaded with slate, waiting for a favourable wind and weather before venturing out into the open sea.

By the time he had reached the position of mate, he had sailed with a number of vessels including the schooner *Ocean Belle, Confidence, Lady Louisa Pennant, Unicorn* and *Mary*. In 1906 he joined the SS *Dora*, used by Robert Owen of 28 Brunswick Road, Liverpool, on its weekly trip with general cargo and a few passengers from Liverpool to Porthdinllaen, Barmouth and Aberdovey, as mate under the command of Captain Robert Lewis before being given command of the SS *Telephone* carrying slate from Caernarfon and Port Dinorwic or Bangor to Liverpool. If there were no slate to be carried, then general cargo would be taken to Aberdovey and Aberystwyth. Captain Roberts served as master with Robert Owen's ships for 25 years, the last ten on the *Christiana* in the coasting and continental trade until 1931 when the company went into liquidation. When he retired in 1932, Captain Roberts had spent 42 years at sea, during which time he served on 26 sailing ships and 9 steamships [UCNW, 11540; *Sea Breezes* 1949 VIII; GAS, XD 15 16/28].

Captain Thomas Wilson Roberts in old age.
[Elsbeth Pritchard]

Captain Thomas Wilson Roberts (1857–1937)

Captain Roberts' sea career started on the schooner, *Venerable*, as a fifteen-year old cook earning four pence a day plus accommodation, such as it was, in the forecastle. Those were the days when every task aboard the sailing vessels, whether it was weighing the anchor, setting sails or unloading the cargo, was carried out by men without the aid of machinery; steam-power was still to come. The ship had a crew of five: the captain, mate, one able seaman, one ordinary seaman and a cook or boy. Straight after getting up in the morning, Thomas Roberts would proceed to the galley, which consisted of a hut 4' square and 5' in height. Inside was a stove with a chimney going through the roof. However, once the stove was alight, the smoke would invariably exit through the door rather than through the chimney causing everything inside the hut including the cook, to be blackened. Whatever state he was in, he was expected to have the kettle boiling and the coffee and sugar added by eight o'clock, otherwise the mate would be none too pleased. In order that there would be no wasting of ingredients, it was the custom to empty the tea kettle but once a week and that was usually on a Sunday afternoon. This resulted in a very strong brew immediately prior to the contents of the kettle being disposed of. When sailors compared ships, it was invariably the quality and quantity of food that mattered rather than the competency of the captain or the workload.

Breakfast was always served in order of seniority, starting with the captain and finishing with the humble cook. It was the mate who was given the responsibility of cooking the midday meal, having had the potatoes and any other vegetable peeled for him. Supper was served at six o'clock prior to a visit ashore. However, such a visit would not be for the boy, unless specially authorised by the mate, who usually specified that, if he went ashore, it would be in the company of the other crew members rather than on his own.

Some of the ship owners, who tended to be penny-pinching, would not only have a reputation for providing poor food, but would also state that a candle, which would be the only means of lighting in the crew's quarters, would only be provided every other night. When he later he joined a three-masted barque, sailing from Cardiff to the Far East, as an able seaman, the rations per week per man were 28 quarts water, 7 lbs bread, 3 lbs salt beef, 2 lbs salt pork, 1 pint peas, 2 lbs flour, $^{1}/_{2}$ lb rice, $1^{3}/_{4}$ oz tea, 4 ozs coffee and 14 ozs sugar. No butter or potatoes were provided. He described the occasional piece of beef provided as being hard enough to model a ship out of it.

On one trip (port of departure not given) to Singapore he describes the flying fish, sharks and other tropical marine life which they encountered. At Singapore, being the first foreign city that he had ever visited, he was aware of the strange language that was being spoken and the fact that the men appeared small in height and with undistinguishable features between each other. They wore just a loin cloth as he said 'which barely covered their nakedness'. He was of the opinion that they lived very cheaply as they 'only ate rice and little of it'. They commenced unloading their cargo of coal on the Sunday morning, with the aid of two baskets at the end of a bamboo pole carried on the shoulder and running along a plank slung between ship and shore. Because of the difficulty in identification and the keeping of records, each man was paid in local currency as each load of coal was brought ashore. With such a method they could work as hard and as long as they wished. All this work was carried out in what Roberts thought was extremely hot weather, having not had such an experience before.

When the unloading was complete the ship sailed with ballast for Bassein but, when they arrived, a member of the crew died, having been ill for a number of days. Since the carpenter was also ill, Roberts was asked to construct a wooden coffin and also to place the body in it. The coffin was then taken ashore and buried without an inquest or any other formality. He described the Cape of Good Hope, which they had to contend with on their voyage home, as a test of the ship as compared with Cape Horn as being a test of the sailor. Before they reached home another member of the crew died and was buried at sea. When they reached Hamburg he decided to leave the ship.

After a period doing coastal work, followed by a trip to the East Indies on board the steamship *Glasgow*, he joined a three-masted steam yacht SS *Pandora* in May 1882 (although Roberts does not give details of the ship's owner or the guests on board, further details from another source are given in Chapter 7 about this voyage), which was sailing to the Arctic as a pleasure cruise. Such a trip entailed a great deal of preparation, not least of all the question of clothes suitable for such a region. The quantity of food put on board was apparently more than was required for the trip. For example, Roberts states that there was enough condensed milk for a thousand people for a year. Of the 40 people on board, 32 were members of crew and the remainder were guests of either the owner of the yacht or of the captain.

In the normal course of events, merchant ships were not allowed to proceed further than 60° N or 60° S, but the yacht had been granted permission to proceed 'To any part of the World where the owner thinks proper'. It was the intention to proceed as far as 88° N on this voyage. She set off north (from her home port of Port Dinorwic) to call at Longhope, in the Orkneys, where the guests on board took the opportunity to do some fishing and later enjoyed eating the catch.

They left after a couple of days and headed for Bergen in Norway, a trip of some 300 miles, where they loaded with food, coal and water. From there they sailed for Hammerfest, which is within the Arctic Circle, before proceeding into the Arctic Ocean where they experienced the midnight sun for the first time. As they proceeded north, and being a short distance from ice, they were suddenly enveloped in a mist. When it cleared, they found themselves solidly lodged in ice. When they extricated the ship, they continued to Hammerfest, from where they proceeded to the White Sea where there was a possibility of observing whales.

At 2am, on the way through a fiord, the vessel struck a submerged rock, even though all hands had been instructed to keep a lookout and they had the benefit of virtually 24 hours of daylight. As a result of the accident, the captain was taken ill and taken ashore where he died. Having disposed of some of her ballast, they managed to get her off the rock with the aid of a passing steamer. All the crew and guests aboard attended the funeral the following day, with the service in the church being conducted in Norwegian and in English at the graveside — apart from a hymn which was sung in Welsh.

After the ballast that was disposed of was replaced and the chief officer was appointed captain, the yacht resumed its previous route, more or less following whalers, to the White Sea. The guests on the yacht were invited on board a whaler, so that they could observe at first hand how they handled the whales after harpooning them. They visited various ports before heading back for Britain in October.

Thomas Roberts continued voyaging on various ships, both sail and steam, until the autumn of 1885, by which time he had reached the position of chief officer and was appointed master mariner three years later.

After a period of sailing various coastal ships he decided to return to Port Dinorwic where he was appointed captain of his 'llong bach' – the *Velinheli*, one of the Dinorwic Quarry steam-ships in 1909. He found sailing during the First World War extremely stressful, since every move that they made sailing from port to port was regulated by Admiralty Controllers. The crew were constantly on the look-out for enemy submarines, which added to the dangers that they encountered, especially as they were not allowed to show any light. He ended his 51 year sailing career, which took him around the world thirteen times, enjoying 15 years with the *Velinheli* followed by being appointed Harbour Master at Port Dinorwic.

Captain Ben Williams (1869–1952)

Captain Ben (as he was known to everyone in the village) was born at Port Dinorwic in 1869, four years after his family had arrived from Nefyn where his father was a sail-maker. When ship-building started at Dinas, he and the family decided to move there in 1865. Since road transport was not readily available for transporting their possessions, they made use of the sailing-ship *Columbia* which had been beached on the sand at Porthdinllaen to make the task of loading easier. However, due to a storm, their departure was postponed until it abated. The delay in not being able to get to his new place of employment meant that there was no income for a whole week which, to a family with five hungry children, caused problems. When they eventually arrived at Port Dinorwic, his mother gave birth to twins, Owen and Robert.

Ben recalled sailing-ships, such as the *Ireland* and *Dusty Miller*,

Captain Ben Williams, photograh taken by J. H. Jones of Port Dinorwic.
[Margaret Tuzuner]

with their cargo of American timber for Caernarfon, being towed along the Strait, but due to her height the *Ireland's* topmast struck the Menai suspension bridge. The development of Port Penrhyn and Port Dinorwic started *c.*1800, a time when very few ships would be seen at either port, but by 1870 there would be a virtual forest of masts at both places. Improvements to the harbour started in 1802, with the building of three berths within the Aberpwll inlet to ease the task of loading ships. The additional berths that were added in 1824, allowed small ships not only to be loaded but, also, to tie up during the winter months when not in use. The work carried out in 1853, which included the

Captain William Morris (Harbour Master at Port Dinorwic) — in the centre holding the small child — and family.   *[Jean Elias]*

reclaiming of further land and the construction of the tidal dock, enabled more dockside to be made available facilitating the task of loading ships.

At the age of twelve, Ben started work at his father's sailroom for six years before going to sea on the *Glan Padarn* which belonged to the Eryri Shipping Company of Llanberis.

Their first voyage was from Liverpool to Rangoon, with 1800 tons of coal, but when they experienced a bad storm, 30 tons of the coal were thrown overboard so as to get a better response from the ship. After rounding the Cape of Good Hope and entering the Indian Ocean, they reached Rangoon, having being at sea four months. When the cargo had been unloaded and the hold cleaned, the ship was loaded with rice for Antwerp. On the way,

Captain William Evans.
[Kathleen Wyn Roberts]

the mate was taken ill and was put ashore at St. Helena. On the second day, after reaching Antwerp, the captain's wife, who had travelled there to meet the ship and her husband, died. Her coffin was brought to Liverpool and eventually taken for burial at Bontnewydd.

Having experienced twelve months of voyaging, Ben decided not to re-engage on the *Glan Padarn*, which was just as well, for she was lost on her next voyage. His second ship was the *Criccieth Castle*, which took a cargo of coal from Cardiff to Callas in Peru, a voyage which took them round the Horn. From Callas they sailed to Pisqua in Chile, where she was loaded with saltpetre for New York. They left there with a general cargo for Melbourne, Australia which took 120 days. The next port of call was Bluff Harbour, New Zealand where they loaded with grain for England but, instead of sailing north, they took an easterly direction so as to take advantage of the prevailing wind and weather. Although he had been away 26 months, he decided to undertake another voyage with the *Criccieth Castle* for which he was paid £4 10s. a month. While sailing between Middlesbrough and Buenos Aires, they experienced a bad cyclone which blew the ship about as if it were a leaf and resulted in the sails being torn to shreds. The person who was responsible for much of the repairs was the ship's carpenter, Robert Williams of Aber Cottages, Port Dinorwic. Whilst crossing the Indian Ocean, they came across the *Cambrian Princess*, owned at one time by Thomas Williams & Company, Menai Bridge, and took the opportunity of exchanging greetings and messages by means of flags. Her carpenter, William Williams, of Islwyn, Port Dinorwic, later attained the rank of master mariner. From Diamond Island, they sailed for Okgah, Japan where she loaded with rice. The six months' voyage had been anything but pleasurable because of food and water shortages. When they arrived back in Britain, and reported to Falmouth, they were told to proceed to Rotterdam where the rice was unloaded.

Mrs Catherine Williams, wife of Captain Ben Williams.   [Margaret Tuzuner]

When Captain Ben returned from his last voyage, which had lasted fifteen months, he decided that future voyages would be short ones. Shortly after his arrival home, Captain William Evans, Glandwr, Port Dinorwic retired as captain of the *Elidir* and Captain Ben took over command. When he eventually retired, he had spent over fifty years at sea.

Many of the retired local captains would 'come ashore' to spend their retirement in the rôle of harbour master. It is believed that the first to be appointed was Captain William Griffith, who had been master of Assheton Smith's yacht *King William* for a period of thirty years. When he retired, the post was filled by his eldest son Thomas Griffith for eighteen years. The maritime connection was severed when the Reverend Morris Hughes was appointed harbour master in 1830.

6. Shipping

Slate, the main commodity exported during the nineteenth and the early part of the twentieth centuries from ports along the Menai Strait, was heavy to both load on to the ship and to store in its hold, nevertheless it could easily be damaged if heavy weather was encountered on a voyage. It was for this reason that the Dinorwic Quarry steamships and, in particular, the SS *Velinheli*, SS *Enid* and SS *Elidir* were specially designed to carry slate. The *Elidir*, largest of the three and considered to be capable of withstanding harsher weather, would undertake the longer voyages and, possibly, the most difficult to Lerwick in the Shetland Isles, Wick, Aberdeen, Peterhead and Fraserburgh. After delivering a cargo of slate, she would occasionally return with ballast of granite from Aberdeen, which would be discarded on to the dockside at Port Dinorwic prior to loading its next consignment of slate. The granite would never be treated as waste. A number of houses in the village, such as those in Terfyn Terrace, were built from such stone. Depending on the distance involved and weather encountered on the voyage, the *Enid* and *Elidir* would aim to undertake an average of two voyages a week. A typical turn round for the *Enid* (Captain Pierce) would be: 10 October, 1928 — Dublin; 16 October, 1928 — Runcorn; 20 October, 1928 — Dublin; 23 October, 1928 — Runcorn; 27 October, 1928 —Preston, with each trip taking 92 tons of slate (during school holidays Captain Pierce would allow his daughter Della and a couple of her friends, whose fathers were also crew members, to be on board for the voyage to Preston).

SS. Velinheli. *[Charles Waine]*

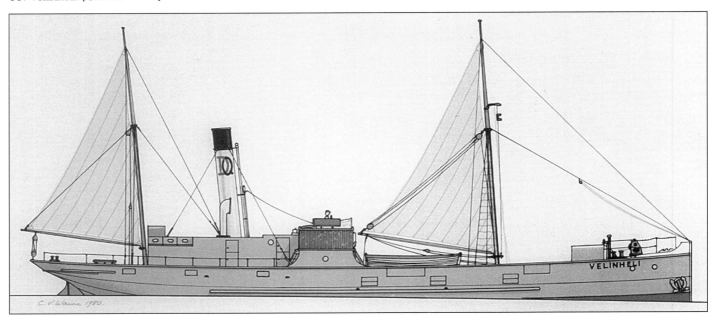

SS Elidir *in working condition, sailing on the Menai Strait. [William Hughes]*

The work pattern for the SS *Velinheli* (Captain Williams), delivering 49 tons of slate on each trip to the nearer ports of Dublin, Preston, Belfast, Birkenhead and Liverpool would be similar but, due to its size, it was not unusual for the SS *Velinheli* to arrive, be loaded and depart on the same tide. Such a turn around was good from a business point of view, but it was very stressful for the captain in particular and, to a lesser extent, the crew. Immediately after the ship had been docked, there would be a rush to get home for clean clothes and fresh food, for which the captain and the crew were responsible for their individual needs. Although ships' crews were allowed double rations during the Second World War compared to the civilian population, replenishing their food store within the time allowed ashore was always a problem. The storing of food on board ship was also difficult since refrigeration was unavailable. Even when stored in a cupboard inaccessible to mice and rats, it tended to deteriorate quickly especially during the summer months.

Such regularity would be virtually impossible for the mostly independently owned smaller schooners, with a capacity of 200 tons or less, since the duration of their voyages would be dependent on the vagaries of the weather. All ships arriving at, and departing from, the slate ports of Porthmadog, Caernarfon, Port Dinorwic and Bangor during the nineteenth century and

SS Enid *at Port Dinorwic being loaded with slate in the traditional way. [Author]*

Slate awaiting shipment at the old harbour, c.1890. Note the number of sailing vessels moored at the quayside. [Gwynedd Archives Service]

Left: The harbour at Port Dinorwic, post 1900. Note the mixture of sail and steam vessels. [Port Dinorwic Historical Society]

Schooners moored at Cei Mawr in the old harbour, c.1910. L–R May Fly, Duke of York, Jane Ann, Helen and Ernest. [Vernon Bowles.

the early part of the twentieth century would be listed in the local newspapers. Those that arrived at Port Dinorwic during the week commencing the 30 June were: *Argo, Annuity, Emily and Louisa, Penmaen, Medway, Lyon, Walter Dean, Virgin, Sarah, Bodicea, Polly Preston, Catherina, William and Mary, Rosa Henrietta, Miss Hunt, Rebecca and Barbara* and the ships that departed during the same week were: *Pearl, Carmarthen, Dinorwic, Aberdeen, Medway, Thomas Jones, Zebra, Emperor, John and Robert, Fritz von Gadow, Sarah Bridget, Progress, Lady Helena and Walter Dean* [*NWC*, 30.6.1883]. The only steam ship that called for slate during that week was the SS *Medway*.

The daily diary from 1884 onwards showed the following movement in and out of Port Dinorwic:

1884
	2 June	*Margaret & Mary** (Capt. Williams) to Arbroth

1885
	6 Jan.	*Galloway Lass* (Capt. Roberts) to Arbroth
	15 Jan.	*Duke of York* (Capt. Mellinger) to Sankey Bridge
	23 Jan.	*Emily Louisa** (Capt. Jones) to Caernarfon
	23 Jan.	*Velinheli* (Capt. Williams) to Liverpool
	4 Feb.	*Dinorwic** (Capt. W M Morris Elias) to Dublin
	18 Feb.	*Venerable* (Capt. Jones) to Middlesborough (Capt. Wilson Roberts, mentioned in Chapters 5 and 7, made his first voyage on this ship)
	20 March	*Menai** (Capt. Williams) to Caernarfon
	23 March	*Why Not* (Capt. Williams) to Caernarfon
	4 April	*Queen of the Isles* (Capt. Bratglas) to Caernarfon
	4 April	*Neptune* (Capt. Roberts) to Caernarfon
	14 April	*Arvon** (Capt. Owens) to Caernarfon
	14 April	*Marquis of Anglesey* (Capt. Griffiths)
	16 April	*Annie* (Capt. Jones) to Hamburg (lost near Strongford Loch 26 October 1892, with all hands)
	30 April	*James* (Capt. Jones) to Caernarfon
	8 May	*Royal Charter* (Capt. Pierce) to Bangor
	22 August	*Mary Rowlands** (Capt. Parry) to Arbroth
	13 October	*Elizabeth Charlotte* (Capt. Jones) to Caernarfon
	23 Nov.	*Minnie Coles* (Capt. Jones) to Caernarfon

(* ships built at Dinas, Port Dinorwic)

1887
	10 Feb.	*Amiable* (Capt. Elias) to Holyhead
	3 Oct.	*Pandora* (Capt. Preston) — Cruising — Vaynol pleasure yacht

1888
	24 Jan.	*Wellington* (Capt. Hughes) to Cadnant (lost 26 May 1897. Capt. Owen Hughes and the mate Owen Roberts drowned)
	15 March	*Brothers* (Capt. Thomas) to Bangor
		Smelter (Capt. Thomas) to Caernarfon
	18 June	*Pandora* (Capt. Bennett) Cruising

1892
	26 Jan.	*Dinorwic* (Capt. Jones) to Kirkcaldy
	12 March	*Elizabeth Bennett* (Capt. Williams) to Dundalk
	14 March	*Velinheli* (Capt. Jones) to Ayr (note in the margin stated that she was in dock from the 5th to the 14th due to a weight dispute which necessitated the cargo being unloaded and reloaded)

Vessels arriving at Port Dinorwic:1885 — 404; 1886 — 403; 1887 — 511; 1890 — 476
Vessels sailing out of Port Dinorwic: 1885 — 390; 1886 — 406; 1887 — 470; 1890 — 489

Movement of vessels out of Port Dinorwic were also recorded by the Caernarfon Harbour Trust and, unless otherwise stated, they were carrying slates. Apart from indicating the names of vessels involved, the register also indicated the name of the captain, tonnages carried and destination [GAS, XD 15-8/8].

SS Velinheli *(right), and other ships (including the* Harlow Plain *— with a striped stack) awaiting loading near the bridge in the new harbour. [Port Dinorwic Historical Society]*

03.12.1887	*Velinheli* (Capt. G. Williams) 65 tons to Liverpool
08.01.1888	*King Ja Ja* (Capt. A. Anderson) 99 tons, goods, to Liverpool
07.02.1888	*Dinorwic* (Capt. I. Elias) 123 tons, goods, to Newry
04.04.1888	*Velinheli* (Capt. G. Griffith) 65 tons, coal, to Preston
29.09.1888	*May Fly* (Capt. M. Atherton) 62 tons to Warrington
17.05.1889	*Arvon* (Capt. H. Roberts) 85 tons to Dundee
19.07.1889	*Virtue* (Capt. O. Huxley) 16 tons, stones, to Nant
11.06.1892	*Elizabeth Bennett* (Capt. J. Williams) 132 tons to Aberdeen
15.06.1892	*Minnie Coles* (Capt. I. Jones) 99 tons to Newcastle
23.06.1892	*Prince Ja Ja* (Capt. A. Anderson) 144 tons, goods, to Liverpool
23.12.1892	*Vaynol* (Capt. I. Jones) 78 tons, coal, from Ayr
23.12.1892	*Mary B. Mitchell* (Capt. J. Jones) 195 tons to Aberdeen
23.03.1901	*Vaynol* (Capt. I. Jones) 78 tons, pig iron, Troon
.03.1903	*St Seiriol* (Capt. H. Parry)
	Velinheli (Capt. Williams), 49 tons, slate, Runcorn
21.04.1901	*Vega* (Capt. Karlssen) 628 tons, timber, from Mobile
1903	*May Fly* (Capt. M. Alerton), 51 tons, slate, Runcorn
.06.1903	*Enid,* (Capt. Wilkins), 40 tons, slate, Glasgow
	Elizabeth Bennett (Capt. Owens), 132 tons, slate, Aberdeen
.08.1903	*Mary B. Mitchell* (Capt. David Davies), 195 tons, slate, Stockton
24.10.1904	*James* (Capt. O. Lewis) 58 tons to Silloth
05.08.1904	*Sarah* (Capt. I. Roberts) 47 tons
19.06.1905	*James* (Capt. O. Roberts) 58 tons to Kirkwall
22.06.1905	*Christiana* (Capt. J. Griffith) 67 tons, goods, from Liverpool

Arrivals and Departures 1906-39 [GAS XD15 — 8/8a–8/9]

21.04.1906	*Pleiades* (Capt. O. Huxley) 12 tons, bricks, to Porthdinllaen
21.12.1908	*Sarah* (Capt. T. Lillie) 47 tons, coal, to Liverpool

Above: Port Dinorwic dry-dock, c.1935. [Author]

Below: Dry-dock workers. [Nancy Tildsley]

01.02.1909	*Harmony* (Capt. S. Chambers) 72 tons to Ayr
07.04.1909	*Sarah* (Capt. T. Lillie) 47 tons, coal, to Liverpool
09.01.1911	*James* (Capt. J. Heaps) 60 tons, coal, to Garston
24.07.1915	*Mary B. Mitchell* (Capt. D. Davies)
20.03.1918	*Helen & Ernest* (Capt. A. P. Arthur) 45 tons
21.03.1920	*Claggan* (Capt. H. Chambers) 59 tons
25.09.1922	*William Sheppard* (Capt. Chambers) 57 tons Beaumaris
27.11.1938	*Alert* (Capt. T. Lillie, owner Lord Anglesey) 132 tons to Port and 01.04.1939
	Dinorwic for refitting

Apart from the Dinorwic Quarry ships: *Enid, Elidir* and *Velinheli*, the only other vessels recorded during the period of the First World War, 1914–18, were the *Tern* (Captain Morris) and *Duke of York* (Captain Plumpton).

From 1919, new vessel names began to appear as well as, possibly, newly appointed master mariners [XD15 16/27]:

Jane Ann (Capt. Pritchard) 57 tons of coal from Runcorn
Pennant (Capt. Owens) 253 tons of slate to Aberdeen
Harlaw Plain (Capt. Williams) 188 tons of slate to Dundee
Elizabeth (Capt. Elias) 46 tons of slate to Runcorn
Elizabeth Charlotte (Capt. Horlock) 116 tons of slate to Dundee
also *Tryfan*, (Capt. Jones), *Protection* (Capt. Hallows), *Alexandra* (Capt. Haughton), *Lady Thomas* (Capt. Evans), *Edith* (Capt. Bennett) together with the *Enid* (Capt. Pierce), *Velinheli* (Capt. Williams), *Elidir* (Capt. Evans), *Roma* (Capt. Brown), *Christiana* (Capt. Roberts) and *Roma* (Capt. Dearden)

SS Pennant, *one of the Penrhyn Quarry fleet, in the dry-dock c.1920.*
[Emyr Wyn Roberts]

Port Dinorwic dock with (L–R): SS Enid, Lizzie, Pennant *(in the dry-dock),* Velinheli *and* Dunmore, *c.1930.*   *[Yvonne Edwards]*

In the latter part of the nineteenth century, and in the years preceding the First World War, the cargoes exported from Port Dinorwic were virtually all slate. The only commodity which was imported on a regular basis was coal and this continued until 1920 when, with the exception of that which the Elidir brought from Boulogne, it got progressively less and less.

Between March and December 1903 amongst the vessels calling at Port Dinorwic were the SS *St Seiriol* (Captain H. Parry), *Velinheli* (Captain Williams), the *May Fly* (Captain M. Alerton), *Enid* (Captain Wilkins), schooner *Elizabeth Bennett* (Captain Owens), *Mary B. Mitchell* (Captain David Davies), *Pandora* (Captain G. Griffiths) and *Elidir* (Captain Thomas Williams) [DQ, XD 15 – 16/8].

Nine years later, in 1912, these vessels, both sail and steam, were carrying slate out of Port Dinorwic [DQ, XD 15 16/22a]:

18 April	*Helen and Ernest* (Capt. Ellis) 37 tons for Runcorn
	May Fly (Capt. Plymton) 51 tons for Sankey Bridge
19 April	*Velinheli* (Capt. Roberts) 49 tons for Dublin
	Enid (Capt. Jones) 110 tons for Weymouth
23 April	*Duke of York* (Capt. Atherton) 46 tons for Runcorn
24 April	*Dinorwic* (Capt. Jones) 11 tons for Weymouth
13 June	*James* (Capt. Lillie) for Weymouth —no tonnage stated
17 June	*Elidir* (Capt. Evans) 99 tons for Aberdeen
22 June	*June and Ann* (Capt. Owen) 57 tons for Newport
19 August	*James* (Capt. Lillie) 58 tons for Douglas
21 August	*Eleanor* (Capt. Jones) 53 tons
12 December	*James* (Capt. Lillie) 58 tons for Douglas

By 1919, it is the Dinorwic Quarry ships *Enid, Velinheli* and *Elidir* which appear most frequently on the shipping register apart from *Tryfan* (Captain Jones), *Protection* (Captain Hallows), *Alexandra* (Captain Haughton), *Lady Thomas* (Captain Evans), *Edith* (Captain Bennett) and *Harlaw Plain* (Captain Williams) [DQ XD 15 16/27].

Compared to steam vessels, sailing vessels were largely at the mercy of the wind, depending on its strength and direction. The task of altering the sails, due to changes in weather conditions, required members of the crew to scramble in an extremely hazardous manner amongst the rigging. The following deposition, expressed by William Roberts, master of the brigantine *Galloway Lass* of Dublin, gives an insight into the difficulties which a sailing ship experienced when sailing within a narrow channel:

104 tons from Runcorn September 25 at 9.30am for Port Dinorwic with 56 tons of coal —Proceeding all well, arriving at Garth Roads, Bangor on the 26th at 10.30am. On 28th at 10.45am tide being high water, weather fine Wind WSW blowing a fresh breeze with a smooth sea from the West, the vessel was beating up the Menai Straits. When off Menai Bridge near the Half Tide Rock, we were standing in to the Anglesea shore with all plain sail set and, whilst in the act of putting the vessel about, she missed stays and struck on the rocks the jib boom striking the end of a house on shore. The vessel then slid up the rock when the bowsprit came in contact with the wall. We then ran out a warp and an anchor on the starboard quarter and hove on it with the windlass, to try and cant her stern in, with the hope her bow would slip off the rock, but all failed. As the tide left, the vessel gradually fell over and is now under water and I fear will become a total wreck. A Trinity pilot was in charge of the vessel at the time but I do not know his number. Menai Bridge Sept. 28th [1886].

According to a report in a local paper, problems could even arise when ships awaited a pilot within the confines of the Strait:

15th October 1886, East Side Swilly Pilot — To the Editor
Sir – I arrived on the 21 June last at 2.45am in the above pilotage waters and made the usual signal. I kept the vessel under way off and on 45 minutes; but not seeing any one coming off to offer his service, came to an anchor, the tide running west until 5am and the vessel being bound to Port Dinorwic with 60 tons of coals, wind NNW light breeze, and fine. On 22nd at 8am a West Side Pilot Nᵒ 3, offered his service, whom I engaged, and proceeded through the Swilly at 11am, arriving at Port Dinorwic Dock at 12.30pm in safety. On the 26th last month I arrived again at 10.30am in the same pilotage waters, and made the Signal for a pilot as before. Light breeze from the westward. At 11am seeing no one appearing except a hobbler whom I refused to take, came to an anchor, the tide running west until 1.30pm which would allow ample time for proceeding through Swilly. The vessel was bound as before with 56 tons of coals to Port Dinorwic. At 4pm this day, fearing that I should not get a Pilot the following morning, I sent the mate to Port Dinorwic to engage one. On 27th nearly throughout the day it blew a gale from SW with heavy rain. At 9am on the 28th I received Nᵒ 3 pilot from West Side, and with the mate and two hobblers to assist, got under way and proceeded for the Swilly. Moderate breeze from the westward. A little east of the Suspension bridge, Anglesea side the vessel stays and grounded on the rocks. At 10pm this night the vessel slipped off the rocks, sank and became a total wreck. I cannot assign any reason for these Pilots not being more attentive unless, on the first occasion, the tide was too early; and secondly it being Sunday. I presume I am not the only one that has been delayed by these pilots. What can be done to prevent such delay.
Yours etc. A Coasting Shipmaster, Port Dinorwic October 12th 1886.
If East Side pilots are not to be found and masters have to take West Side pilots complaint should be made to the Pilotage authority.

Even when the ship had the benefit of steam, she was still at the mercy of the weather as shown in the following account:

The report submitted by Robert Owen, master of the schooner rigged screw steamer *Tolfaen* of and from Liverpool 99 tons Oct 4th at 10pm for Newry with 183 tons wheat. On the 5th at 3 am, the tide half ebb weather clear wind NW by W strong and squally with a cross sea from the NW, the vessel was proceeding with about 60lb of steam head to wind Great Ormes Head bearing SW about 10 miles distant, when a heavy cross sea struck the vessel on the starboard side

about the fore rigging, which threw her on her beam ends and shifted the cargo. The mate, two able seaman and a lad and engineer, thinking the vessel was going down, made for the boat. Another heavy sea came right over and washed me off my feet, through the alleyway and nearly overboard and when I recovered I found the boat and the five men gone. Myself and the firemen managed with great difficulty to get vessel before the wind and she nearly foundered several times. We then managed to get the vessel into Rhos Bay and let go our anchor about 6am. I then hoisted signals of distress, and the Llandudno Lifeboat came off and assisted to trim portion of cargo and four of the lifeboat's crew assisted me to bring the vessel to Bangor. In my opinion, portion of the cargo must be damaged, the vessel having 4 feet of water in her hold. Bangor, October, 1888.

Until the advent of steamships, slate, brought down from the quarries to the nearest port, was exported by a variety of sailing vessels of fifteen tons and upwards e.g.:

Elizabeth (12386), 37 tons, registered in 1856, capable of carrying a variety of cargo including slate from ports such as Pwllheli, Caernarfon and Port Dinorwic. In 1864 the owner and master was given as Richard Owen of Nefyn. Forty years later she was owned and captained by John Huxley Hughes, 50 Chapel Street, Caernarfon, with a crew which included Owen Huxley, who was later to serve on the *Virtue*.

Dinorwic (44234) — a three-masted, 99 ton, wooden schooner 80.3' x 22.0' x 11.5', built in 1862 by Rees Jones & Son at Dinas, Port Dinorwic and used mostly to carry slates. She was owned by Robert Griffith, 10 Chapel Street, Caernarfon and her master was Captain J. O. Griffiths. Amongst the crew were William Cale and John Pritchard, both of whom were from Bangor and had served on the *Elizabeth Bennett*. The *Dinorwic* was torpedoed in 1917.

Arvon (28541) 1863–99 — in the ownership of Captain Owen Owens, Halfway House, Port Dinorwic from 1872 until 1892 when he sold it to Captain W. Parry, 15 Castle Street, Caernarfon. When Captain Owens was not on board, as master of the vessel, it would be under the control of Captain William Parry together with Frances Jones (mate), Theophilus Jones and Robert Ellis (able seamen).

Polly Preston (47753) — a schooner of 98 tons, measuring 89.6' x 22.6' x 11.7', registered in 1863 at Caernarfon. She was owned by Robert Preston and master was Captain Evan Davies.

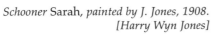

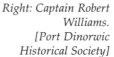

Left: Captain H. D. Parry, c.1935.
[Yvonne Edwards]

Right: Captain Robert Williams.
[Port Dinorwic Historical Society]

She carried on average a crew of nine men. By June 1887, ownership had been acquired by L. Williams & Son, Florence Terrace, Port Dinorwic and the master was Captain David Williams, Port Dinorwic. The following year Lewis Williams continued as owner, but his son Captain Robert Williams had been appointed as master. By 1898 and for the next four years, the owner was shown as Hugh Owen, Cefn Farm, Port Dinorwic and master as Captain Robert Williams.

Sarah (1501) (1871–79) — registered at Caernarfon in 1871 and owned by Robert Owen. Those who served on her included Captain Robert Hughes, Captain Hugh Jones and Captain David Pugh. She was wrecked on Rhyl beach in October 1879.

James (10278) — 58 tons, members of the crew sailing the schooner *James* (58 tons) were generally from Port Dinorwic and Caernarfon and included: Captain John Huxley Hughes (1904); Captain John Jones, 3 Menai Street, Port Dinorwic; Mate — John Roberts (December 1892); Owen Huxley (July 1872); William Evans (December 1896); Andrew Maguire (June 1896); Charles Bowles (December 1899); Jeremiah Davies (who had been a mate on the *Christiana* in 1903). Having been a crew member of a variety of vessels including the *Sarah*, Thomas Lillie became the captain of the *James* when he bought the vessel for £300 from Mrs Apollonia Roberts, 3 Glandŵr Terrace, Bangor on 25 August 1910. Amongst those who subsequently crewed her were: Owen John Elias, Hugh Roberts, Peter Dop, Jenkin Thomas Williams, John Davies (who had served on the SY *Amalthea*), Owen Richard Williams, Thomas John Lillie (Thomas Lillie's son), Robert James Bowles, Hugh David Parry, John Dop, Hugh Dop (the latter two had served on the *St. Trillo*).

Schooner James, *painted by J. Jones, c.1908.*
[Harry Wyn Jones]

The original Velinheli, *tied up at Greystones, Ireland, October 1910. She was built at Dinas, Y Felinheli in 1877.*
[Derek Paine]

Virtue (70313) (1876–1913), a smack of 16 tons gross, mostly carried sand and lime. Her owner in 1882 was Henry Hughes, Glandon, Caernarfon with Owen Huxley, Pool Hill, Caernarfon as master. By 1913, David Pierce, Frondeg, Port Dinorwic had taken her over as both owner and master and had with him John Pierce Jones, also of Port Dinorwic, as mate. She carried a variety of cargo between Caernarfon, Porthdinllaen, Port Dinorwic, Beaumaris, Trefor, Parkia Brick Works and Lewis Wharf Bangor. After being employed as a carpenter during the construction of the Britannia Bridge, John Pierce Jones (1825–1907), a native of Llanfair PG, went to live in Port Dinorwic and to work as a carpenter on local ships being built at Dinas. In time, he became the owner of four small ships: the *Royal Charter, Neptune, Harmony* and the *Virtue* (on which he had at one time served as mate) used mostly to bring sand across from Chwarel Goch in Anglesey, at a time when there was much building work being carried out at Port Dinorwic in the second half of the nineteenth century.

Velinheli (80227) (1878–1909), the first vessel to carry this name was a two-masted 65 ton schooner built at Dinas, Port Dinorwic in 1878 by Rees Jones & Co. Measuring 75.2′ x 21.3′ x 9.3′, she had an elliptic stern and was of carvel construction (registered at Caernarfon 21 October 1878). During the period between 1878–1909 she was owned and managed by John Dean, a slate merchant of Blackburn. Her first master in 1878 was 51-year-old G. Williams of 3 Bodlondeb Terrace, Port Dinorwic. His crew was John Jones (mate) and John Thomas and Rowland Pritchard (able seamen). By 1888, Griffith Griffiths had taken over as master, followed by Thomas M. Williams in 1890, and James Hollingworth the following year. She carried slate and coal between north Wales ports and Fleetwood, Liverpool, Peterhead, Aberdeen, Ipswich and Plymouth. She was sold by John Dean on 27 May, 1891 to Arthur Evans, coal merchant, of Greystones, Co. Wicklow, Ireland, for £850, with the transaction being registered at the Custom House, Caernarfon. We are able to follow some more of her history from a report printed in the *Irish Times* on 14 October, 1910, concerning a bad storm which had occurred at Greystones:

> Three small schooners, the *Velinheli* of Greystones (owned by Mr Arthur Evans), the *Federation* and the *Reciprocity* were moored on Wednesday night by the East Pier, but by half past four yesterday morning, the cables of all three vessels parted, having been unable to bear the severe strain of the high seas which rushed into the harbour and over the East Pier. The crew of the *Velinheli* wisely abandoned the vessel, by scrambling along the bowsprit and dropping on to the pier wall.

Even so, the *Velinheli* survived the storm and continued trading until she was eventually lost, after a collision with the Blue Funnel ship *Laertes* of Liverpool in fog in Liverpool Bay 25 January, 1915. Once

Engineer John Roberts (in his Royal Naval Reserve uniform) and his family, c.1900. [Betty Pierce Jones]

again the crew of four: Captain Hollensworth, Mr Byrne, Mr Cleary and Mr Hunt (and the cat) were rescued.

Dinorwic (92205) With increasing demand for slate and the need for a more efficient method of delivery, G. W. D. Assheton-Smith, of Vaynol and owner of the Dinorwic Quarry, decided to replace the sailing ships, used to deliver his slate, with steamships. The first to be built by S. McKnight & Co., Ayr in 1892, was the *Dinorwic* (111 tons) 128' x 23' x 10.4'. The owner's name was given as the Hon. W. W. Vivian, Plas Dinorwic, who managed the estate on behalf of Assheton Smith. The 1892 crew was listed as Master: Captain Thomas Williams together with Thomas John Jones, John Roberts, Andrew Maguire, William Caddock, Thomas Wilson and Evan Hughes (who had previously served on the first *Velinheli*). The captain in 1898 was Captain J. Roberts.

Other crew members listed over the years, some of whom were to become master mariners, were Edward M. Williams (mate); Richard Pritchard (engineer); Daniel Davies (leading fireman); John Roberts and Owen J. Elias (firemen), the latter had previously been on the *James*; William Evans (able seaman); John Jones (able seaman); Owen Jones (able seaman); Hugh G. Owens (able seaman), the latter had previously served on the *Velinheli*; Owen Donaldson (cook); Llewelyn Pritchard (cook); William Jones (cook); Robert Pierce (cook). Typically, the voyages undertaken by the *Dinorwic* were with slate to Middlesborough, Dublin, Boston (Lincolnshire), Hull and Newcastle-upon-Tyne.

Velinheli (102641), the second steamship to be purchased by Assheton Smith in 1892 and the second vessel to bear the name. She was built by S. McKnight & Co., of Ayr. Owing to a dispute between Assheton Smith and the shipbuilder, he refused to accept her and she was sold to another company and named *Dunlossit*. When the dispute was settled, she was eventually bought by Assheton Smith in 1894 and renamed *Velinheli*. She delivered slate from Port Dinorwic for a period of some 47 years sailing to Preston, Ireland, Runcorn and Liverpool, where she would often transfer her cargo to ocean-going vessels. She was one of the smallest (49 tons) of the Dinorwic Quarry Co. purpose built slate carriers, measuring 95' x 18.5' x 7.5'. Her 40hp compound engine enabled her to attain a speed of $9^1/_2$ knots. Accommo-dation was provided for the captain, mate and two engineers beneath the bridge, whilst two

Mary B. Mitchell *under sail.*
[Emyr Wyn Roberts]

The crew of the Mary B. Mitchell. *[Ivor Rees]*

seamen and two firemen shared the forecastle. The fore and aft sails appear to be a relic of the days before steam, although it was said that that they were useful, provided the captain had had previous experience under canvas. Amongst those who served on her were: Captain J. H. Jones, Captain Thomas Wilson Roberts and Captain Williams, T. E. Hughes, Robert Pierce, William Evans, Thomas Pritchard, Thomas Jones, William Jones, Hugh Williams, Robert Caddock, William Caddock, Isaac Jones, Ellis Edwards and Owen Roberts.

Vaynol (92210) (1892–1902), 79 tons, measuring 129' x 22' x 7.7', was built in 1892 by S. McKnight & Co., Ayr, for the Dinorwic Quarry Co. and had a 45hp engine. Her master was Captain John H. Jones, 3 Menai Street (later Bush Cottage), Port Dinorwic. She was in service for a period of ten years before sinking in the Mull of Galloway, as a result of a collision.

Mary B. Mitchell (97575). The shipyard of Paul Rogers & Co., at Carrickfergus in Northern Ireland had already established a reputation for building fine ships when Owen Thomas Jones, of Erw Fair, Bangor, managing owner of the Anglesey Shipping Co., placed an order for a steam ship Nᵒ· 34 as she was listed at the shipyard. She was launched on 18 October, 1890, and named SS *Anglesey*. Her competitive price of £2,700 was intended to attract further orders and this it succeeded in doing. The vessel, with its dimensions of 99' x 18' x 8¹/₂' and an average speed of 9¹/₂ knots, had been specially built for carrying about 130 tons of slate.

The next vessel that O. T. Jones ordered the following year, laid down as Nᵒ· 38 at the shipyard, was a 227-ton three-masted, steel-hulled, topsail schooner measuring 129' x 24' x 11', surveyed at Belfast and registered at Beaumaris. Subsequent to her being launched by a Miss Florrie Turpin of Belfast, and being named the *Mary B. Mitchell* on 30 March 1892, she carried a cargo of rock salt on her maiden voyage, under the command of Captain T. Williams to Bangor in north Wales (the 1896 *Sailing Register* gave the owner's name as W. M. Preston with O. T. Jones as manager).

Her arrival at Port Penrhyn on the Easter Monday, bedecked in bunting and under tow from the steamer *Anglesey*, was greeted by a large crowd which had gathered at Garth and Hirael. The very high standard of fittings throughout the vessel, and of the accommodation for both the officers and men, and the fact that she could sail without ballast, gave her the appearance of being more suitable for private use rather than a slate carrier.

By the 30 June 1893 of the following year, the Ship's

Mary B. Mitchell under sail and looking the worse for wear.
[Ivor Rees]

Agreement stated that the master was Captain J. Jones of Port Dinorwic and mate Griffith Rees. Rees' wife Ann (1837–1930) not only raised a family and was a midwife in Port Dinorwic, but also found time to sign on occasionally as a cook so as to sail with her husband. One voyage that she undertook soon after launching, was when a delivery of slate was being made to Newcastle on 24 January, 1893. The return voyage, with a variety of cargoes picked up along the way, took them to London, Dublin, Bangor, Hamburg, London and ended in Port Dinorwic on 13 June, 1893. Such a voyage would be typical of the work that the *Mary B. Mitchell* and similar vessels undertook, with the length of the voyage dependent on work available and cargoes to be delivered.

While bound for Hamburg, with slate, the *Mary B. Mitchell* went aground at Texal Bank, Holland on 27 December, 1896. The crew were taken off before she became badly damaged and sank. She was re-floated on the 18 January, 1897 and repaired before being sold in 1898 to E. A. Young. She was once again involved in an accident while anchored in Weymouth Roads on the 31 January, 1903, when, struck by HMS *Hogue*, she lost her bowsprit and her stern was damaged.

During the First World War, the *Mary B. Mitchell* was requisitioned by the Admiralty (5 May 1916) and used as a Q-ship with Lieutenant M. Armstrong, RNR, in command. Armed with one 12lb gun, two 6lb guns and two Lewis guns, she sailed under a variety of names including *Mitchell*, *Q-9* and *Mary y José*. She was sold in 1919 for £6,500 and took part in several films before being used in the Irish Sea coal trade. Her days ended on 15 December 1944 when, on a voyage from Dublin to Shilloth with a cargo of burnt ore, she was driven ashore in a gale at Torrs Point near Kirkcudbright and was wrecked. The crew of eight were saved by the local lifeboat [UCNW, BC 37089 (inc) 97575].

Enid (118501), 45 tons, was built by the Ailsa Shipbuilding Co. in August 1903 for G. W. Assheton Smith. She had two masts rigged fore and aft and measured 131.5' x 22.35' x 10.45'. Her engine was built by Ross & Duncan, Glasgow and was capable of 9 knots. The crew listed in 1903 were: Master – Thomas Jones (previously with the *Vaynol*); Mate – William Evans (previously with *Dinorwic*); Mate – William Jones; Mate – Thomas Hughes (previously *Dinorwic*); Engineer – Thomas Hughes (previously *Vaynol*); Engineer – Andrew Maguire (previously *Alistair*); 2nd Engineer – Griffith Evans; AB – William Jones (previously *Velinheli*); AB – John Lewis (previously *St Tudwal*); AB – Edward Roberts; Fireman – John Roberts; AB – Owen Pritchard; AB – William Pierce (previously *Dinorwic*); Fireman – John Davies (previously *Marguerite*). By 1904, the following changes had been made to the crew: Master — John Jones; Mate — E. Hughes; Engineer — Thomas Hughes; Engineer — Daniel Davies; AB — John Lewis; AB — William Pierce; AB — John Jones; AB — William Jones; Fireman — John Davies; Fireman — John Jones; Fireman — Richard Williams.

Other Master Mariners involved with the *Enid* and other Dinorwic Quarry ships were Captain J. Jones, Captain Owen John Jones, Captain Hugh David Parry, Captain Robert Pierce and Captain William David Williams.

Typical voyages that she would undertake were:
1 January [c.1935] depart Port Dinorwic for Glasgow

SS Enid *on the Mersey en route to Port Dinorwic.*
[William Hughes]

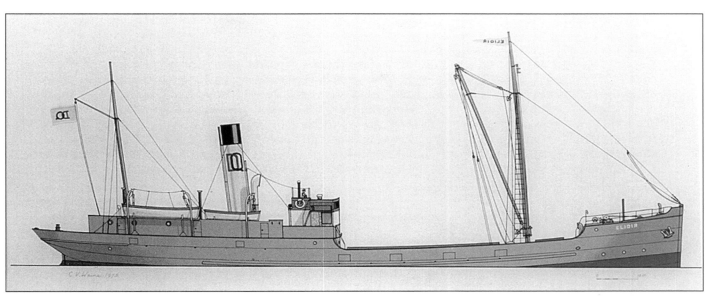

SS Elidir. *[Charles Waine)*

2 January depart Glasgow for Belfast
3 January arrive Port Dinorwic
5 January depart for Swansea
18 January depart for Swansea
19 January arrive Swansea
23 January depart Llanelli
24 January arrive Port Dinorwic
25 January depart Port Dinorwic
26 January arrive Belfast

Vessels employed in the slate trade and trading between Port Dinorwic and the rivers Mersey, Dee and Clyde, Fleetwood, Solway Firth, Dublin, Belfast and London would average two trips a week.

The *Enid*, the last of the Dinorwic Quarry ships to act as flagship for the local regatta, was put on sale September 1942 with Thomas McLaren & Co., Glasgow for £7,500 but, due to war-time regulations which stated that any sale would be conditional on the ship remaining in home waters, she remained with the company until after the war, when she was sold to the Hammond Lane Metal Co. Ltd., Dublin, for scrap.

Elidir (118502), 99 tons, was built in 1903 for G. W. D. Assheton Smith as part of his Dinowic Quarry fleet of slate carriers by S. McKnight & Co., Ayr, shipyard (later to be known as the Ailsa Shipbuilding Co.). She had a 91hp engine and measured 151.6′ x 25.1′ x 9.9′ and would undertake the longest voyages from Port Dinorwic round the north of Scotland to Aberdeen and Wick. She could accommodate thirteen men if necessary. She first arrived at Felinheli on 7 September 1903 and left fully loaded three days later.

The first master to serve on the Elidir was Captain Thomas Williams with Thomas Wilson Roberts as mate. Other members of the crew were: Mate — Edward Martin Williams; Mechanics — A. Doyle, Henry R. Pierce, Charles Bowles, Griffith Jones and John Owen; Leading Fireman — Andrew Maguire; Fireman — Owen Williams; Fireman — John Roberts; Cook — John T. Jones; Cook — Robert D. Vaughan.

Although Thomas Wilson Roberts is recorded as being Master in 1906, it

Walter Palmer. [Port Dinorwic Historical Society]

is Captain Thomas Williams who hands over command of the *Elidir* to Captain William Evans on 12 October, 1909. His crew in 1910 were listed as Mate — Edward M Williams; AB — Hugh Pritchard; AB — Thomas J. Williams; Cook — Johnnie Hughes; Engineer — Richard Pritchard; Engineer — Andrew Maguire; Fireman — Griffith Jones; Fireman — Daniel Davies; Fireman — John Roberts (who had previously been with the SY *Amalthea*); Fireman — Owen Donaldson (previously *Dinorwic*).

In 1913, whilst delivering slate to Stockton-on-Tees, the following report was filed by the captain in the ship's log:

At 11.30am found Andrew Maguire (born at Penrhyn, Cornwall) second engineer in his bed, dead, my attention drawn to this occurrence by Griffith Jones, fireman. I at once sent for the police, who came on board at midday and removed the body to the mortary [sic] inquest was held today 20 inst – balance of wages due £2.1/-.

The inscription on his gravestone reads — 'Andrew Maguire husband of Ellen J. Maguire, 21 Snowdon Street, Port Dinorwic died on board SS *Elidir* at Stockton-on- Tees 19.10.1913 age 50'.

Whilst on a voyage with a cargo of slate, the *Elidir* ran aground in thick fog near Fraserburgh. Although extensively damaged, she managed to proceed to the intended port of Kirkcaldy where she was able to discharge her cargo. On her return to Port Dinorwic, the damage to her hull was inspected in the dry-dock and, although Lloyd's Insurance was of the opinion that she was a total loss, with a market value of £3,000, the decision was taken to repair her at the dry-dock at the eventual cost of just over £10,000.

After serving as a mate, Owen J. Jones took command of the *Elidir* in 1933 and amongst his crew were Griffith Evans as Chief Engineer [HRO D/CK/24 - 1942] and Goronwy Owen as fireman (from April 1941 to January 1944). Due to the general slump in trade during the 1930s which also affected the slate industry, it was necessary for ships like the *Elidir* to look elsewhere for cargoes. As a result, she would spend up to six months at a time on the east coast of England carrying coal to London and returning with iron ore. She would only return to Port Dinorwic when she was due for routine maintenance such as boiler cleaning.

A letter, sent by the Quarry Manager to Captain Jones of the *Elidir* and Captain Parry of the *Enid*, gives an indication of the rate of pay that the men were subjected to during the period of the war and the attitude of the management:

6.2.1942 to Capt. Owen J Jones, SS *Elidir* … all the men on board the SS *Elidir* with the exception of yourself, engineer and mate are to receive 5/- per week overtime … [DQ 2807b]

An incident which occurred during this period caused O. T. Williams, general manager of the Dinorwic Quarry Co. to send a letter to Brodrick, Leitch & Kendall of Liverpool: 'SS *Elidir* … whilst entering the Alfred Lock at Birkenhead … collided with the Alfred Pier Head and as a result fractured the port hawse pipe …' The cost of repairs was later assessed at £96 18s.6d.

By 1942, the number of slates being produced under war-time conditions were delivered either by rail or road without resorting to the obvious dangers of sailing. Consequently, Captain Jones' last cargo was that of salt from Runcorn to Glasgow returning to Connahs Quay in ballast. When he retired from sailing, the reference that he received from the General Manager stated:

25.03.1943 This is to certify that Mr Owen John Jones, Snowdon Street, Port Dinorwic has served on the SS *Elidir* as Captain from November 5th 1939 until May 2nd 1943 when the ship was sold. During the said period ,he gave entire satisfaction in all ways …

RSS Harlow Plain *entering Barrow-in-Furness, 21 March 1924, under the command of her owner, Captain Ben Williams. [Emyr Wyn Roberts]*

When he 'came ashore' Captain Jones was appointed Harbour Master at Port Dinorwic.

As a result of the Coppack Brothers (Connah's Quay) ship *Farfield* being sunk by a German aircraft off Bardsey Island in 1941, the company purchased the *Elidir* from the Dinorwic Quarry Co. Ltd. in 1942. Immediately after, she was requisitioned by the Admiralty and used between 30 November 1943 and May 1944, in what was described as 'Miscellaneous Military' activities which, initially, meant she was used for commando training. Having relocated her mast and lengthened her main hatch, further alterations were carried out at Liverpool to the crew's quarters, in November 1942, at a cost of £661 19s. 6d. and fitting rolling chocks [the means of securing cargo or articles on deck to prevent movement in rough seas] in August 1943 to improve stability at a cost of £544 13s. 4d.

At the time of the D-Day landings in Normandy, the *Elidir* sailed as part of Convoy ETC3W 9th, from the Thames, via the Solent, to the Gold sector of the Normandy beaches. She also participated by taking

SS Elidir *moored at the Mulberry Harbour off the D-Day landing beaches, Normandy, June 1944. [Emyr Wyn Roberts]*

Captain Walter W. Horlock and his son (of the same name).
[Steve Williams]

supplies across the Channel and landing them on the Mulberry Harbour in Normandy, and to Dieppe, Ostend and Caen, before eventually returning to Southampton [FRO, D/CK/861]. During the period when she was involved with the Normandy landings, she was under the command of Captain Edward A. Bennett; Arthur Bennett and B. Evans alternated as Chief Engineer, J. V. Prince was Mate and W. Palmer 2nd Engineer. The other crew members were Able Seaman A. Yates; Firemen W. Jellicoe, T. P. Owen and A. Farrigia; Ordinary Seaman V. Spark together with two gunners [FRO D/CK/281].

After such a varied service, the *Elidir* was broken up for scrap in 1955.

Harlow Plain, 462 tons and measuring 150.1' x 25.2' x 10' was built by J. Lewis & Son in Aberdeen in 1921 as a replacement for the SS *Alistair*. Captain Ben Williams (1876–1952) was in command of her from the time when she was launched until 1931. Amongst his crew were Walter Horlock, Richard Dop, William Favretto, John Jones, Richard Thomas and Robert David Howard. A typical voyage for the *Harlow Plain* was to carry slate from Port Dinorwic to Aberdeen, then a cargo of coal to Ireland. She was eventually sold to a company in France and renamed *Cherbourg*.

Veronica Tennant, 397 tons, launched in 1922 as the *Ipswich Trader* but not fully fitted out as the builders, Colby Brothers of Lowestoft, ceased trading. In 1928 she was completed by the Mistley Shipbuilding & Repair Co. for the owner F. W. Horlock and, in 1935, lengthened by 20' to 142' x 24.1' x 10.6'. She was sold to Duff, Herbert & Mitchell in 1946 and renamed *Veronica Tennant*. She was broken up at Llanelli in 1954.

Seiont and *Seiont II*. Although Caernarfon and Felinheli's maritime connection was declining by the early part of the twentieth century, the sea traffic was sufficiently heavy to justify having a dredger to ensure that the harbours and approaches to the ports were kept clear of the ever encroaching mud. Without that periodical clearance, vessels which carried slate from Port Dinorwic and Caernarfon would have great difficulty negotiating narrow channels. This also applied to the regular callers bringing goods on a weekly basis from Liverpool or visitors aboard the pleasure steamers also from Liverpool, Llandudno or Menai Bridge.

The dredger Seiont II *moored in the Victoria Dock, Caernarfon. [Author]*

Shell Trader passing under the Menai suspension bridge after unloading at Caernarfon. [Emyr Wyn Roberts]

The original vessel allocated with the task of mud clearance was the *Seiont*, but by the 1930s it had outlived its usefulness. To justify its disposal to a Birkenhead firm for the sum of £145, the Caernarvon Harbour Trust stated in a report to a local paper in February 1939 that the old vessel had mostly tended buoys rather than clear mud. The new vessel which was called *Seiont II* and described on the Certificate of Registry as a 'steel grab hopper barge', was built by W. J. Yarwoods of Northwich and arrived at Caernarfon 8 November 1937. She was 86′ 7″ in length with a beam of 20′ 1″, weighed approximately 125 tons and cost £7,874. Her coal-fired 160 bhp compound engine gave her a speed of approximately 8 knots. She continued dredging until 1978 when she was taken out of service. Since she was the only ship of her kind in Wales and one of very few in the UK in working order at that time, enthusiasts decided that she should be saved and not scrapped. The National Museum of Wales was approached and not only agreed to purchase it from the owners, the Caernarfon Harbour Trust, but also to pay for a complete overhaul and necessary renovations. In the spring of 1990, the National Museum of Wales decided to sell the *Seiont II* for a nominal sum to a society called 'The Seiont II Maritime Trust' (*Ymddiriedolaeth Forol Seiont II*). Subsequent repairs carried out to the ship, costing in excess of £12,000, were paid for by grants from organisations such as the Science Museum in London, the Council for Museums in Wales and the Welsh Church Acts Fund and the shortfall covered by monies raised by members of the Trust.

In 1992, *Seiont II* was presented with a marine award in the form of a framed certificate and the sum of £1,000 at the Beamish Open Air Museum by Steam Heritage, an organisation backed by British Coal. The award was an apt testimonial to the enthusiasm and hard work of the volunteers who maintained the working exhibit. In addition, the Trust was also responsible for the Maritime Museum on Victoria Dock in Caernarfon, with its artefacts and memorabilia pertaining to the *Seiont II* in particular and to maritime matters generally.

Sadly, this handsome but well worn vessel, subjected over the years to all weathers and the corrosive effect of sea water, saw its boilers, which also suffered from the ravages of work and time, having the original working pressure of 135psi being reduced to around 20psi. Even the occasional jaunt down the Strait by members of the society, with a picnic on deck and a bridge-full of 'not-so-qualified' would-be helmsmen under the supervision of a master mariner, became an impossible task when the old *Seiont* could not even fight against an adverse tide. Eventually, the decision was taken that the leaking hull and wafer-thin stack could not be maintained any longer, even by the dedicated supporters. The sad day eventually came when she was taken to Penrhyn port in 1999 to be broken up.

The Dinorwic Quarry Co. purchased a number of second-hand coasters after the war including the *Dawlish*, *Alfred Mason* and *Juliet Duff*. Although the latter was managed by Mr O. T. Williams, who had charge of all the quarry ships, she was registered in the name of Duff, Herbert & Mitchell Ltd. and carried their colours. By 1956, only the ageing *Sybil Mary*, shortly to be sold, remained.

The Dinorwic Quarry, for various reasons, did not recover their pre-war level of activity or marketing capability. Even if the quarry sheds at Llanberis had not been requisitioned for aircraft production (NECACO) in 1940, it is hardly likely that slate would have been produced in pre-war quantities, either during or after the war. Whereas Welsh slate, considered to be the best in the world and without equal, had been exported for some two hundred years, the post-war period saw slate being imported because of cheaper prices.

7. Sailing and Regattas

Until the early part of the twentieth century, yachting on the Menai Strait was very much the prerogative of wealthy individuals who were mostly local land owners. The vessels involved ranged from true sailing yachts, of between 19 and 25 tons, to steam vessels which varied in size from 100 to 1,000 tons. These latter vessels were capable of, and in fact were used for, long distance cruising. The racing yacht that would have been seen on the Strait in the nineteenth century and the early part of the twentieth, would be in complete contrast to that which evolved from the 1930s. Not only did the design and size of yacht change, there was also a change in ownership: from being an exclusive club enjoyed by the rich, it became the hobby of many and the not-so-rich.

Glynllifon

In keeping with the style of the period, the Newborough family was also involved in boating and yachting. Although Glynllifon, the family seat in Llandwrog, was a couple of miles from the sea, they had the benefit of nearby Fort Belan with its accommodation and private harbour which allowed easy access into the Menai Strait. Some of the vessels owned by the family during the nineteenth century were the *Arvon, Maria Stella, Sapphire, St.*

Fort Belan, at the southern entrance to the Menai Strait. The dock can be seen top centre of the picture. [Author]

David's, Bardsey Isle, Llyfon, Firefly, Vesta, Mira and *Birdie* and, in the early part of the twentieth century, the ocean-going steam yacht *Mora*. The *Mira*, a 329 ton steel, steam yacht (154' x 21.5' x 12.5') built by D. J. Dunlop at Glasgow and with an engine producing 50hp, was purchased by the Hon. Frederick Wynn in the late summer of 1891. He was possibly motivated by an element of competition from his contemporaries, such as Assheton Smith's SY *Pandora* and Sir Richard Bulkeley's SY *Aphrodite*.* When speed trials on the *Mira* were being carried out between Kingston, Ireland and Holyhead, they had on board Mr J. P. Winton, a builder of marine and static engines at the Union Foundry in Caernarfon. Although he was not responsible for the construction of the engine, he had been invited on board because of his expertise in matters of marine engines and, in particular, the excessive vibration being experienced on the *Mira* when travelling at a speed of 15 knots. It was eventually proved that it was being caused by the three-bladed propeller and was rectified when this was changed to a four-bladed one, as recalled by a member of the crew in a letter published in the 1930s. The same letter writer suggested that the Hon. Frederick Wynn was not an enthusiastic sailor, even though the *Mira* was quite capable of voyaging far and wide. The commander of the vessel at this time was Captain David Elias, the coxswain was John Davies and Evan Jones, William Roberts and John Roberts were the other crew members. When necessary, members of the Glynllifon staff, irrespective of their normal duties, were liable to be enrolled on board to supplement the normal crew.

Plas Newydd

Plas Newydd, the beautifully situated home of the Earl of Uxbridge (who became the Marquess of Anglesey in 1815) on the banks of the Menai Strait, had direct access to its own private harbour. In 1787/88, the family owned the yachts *Mona* and *Druid* which were crewed by James Dean (mate), M. McKenzie and Griffith Davies (the captain's name is unrecorded). Apart from the crew's wages, typical bills paid during one trip were:

> Pilotage from Park Gate to Chester £1 5/-; 2 January 1788 Dr Edwards' bill for attending the Boys when sick £3 4/-; Feb 1 1788 Thomas Danson for Castle Dues at the Island of St Mary's Scilly 1/6d; Feb 3 Piloting the *Mona* in and out of Scilly 15/- then on to Falmouth, Plymouth, Dover and London; Spirits bought for the crew @ 6/6d a gallon; 3 August 1788 Evan Jones, Pilot from Carnarvon to Plas Newydd 5/- [Plas Newydd, Series II, 3487].

Problems may have been anticipated on certain voyages, possibly from pirates, since included in the equipment carried on board the yacht were 4 muskets, 1 blunderbuss, 4 bayonets, 6 cutlasses and a pair of pistols [PN 3489] (see Appendix IV).

The *Pearl*, a 42-ton yacht built by P. Sainty of Colchester and captained in its early days by James Saunders, was launched in 1820 and retained by the 1st Marquess until his death in 1854. In the typical style of the sailing fraternity, the greater part of the summer of 1823 was spent by the Marquess and his family, voyaging along the south coast and visiting a number of ports, including Cowes, during the yachting season. While visiting Southampton on the 23 June, Admiral the Hon. Sir Charles Paget joined other guests on board the *Pearl*. On the 3 August, the Marquess extended a challenge to 'Mr Smith' (he may well have been Thomas Assheton Smith, his neighbour at Vaynol) to a race round the Isle of Wight for 1,000 guineas and he would be given the benefit of a 4-mile start. Whether the challenge was accepted or not is not known (both the Marquess and the Assheton Smith's were members of the Royal Victoria Yacht Club, Ryde, Isle of Wight) [PYA 29106].

*It appears that *Aphrodite* was acquired by Assheton Smith by 1905–6 [VP 4635].

SY Oimara *anchored in the Menai Strait off Plas Newydd. [National Trust]*

The Lloyds Register for 1888, indicates that Lord Anglesey owned the *Santa Cecilia* (85075) a 96-ton steam yacht 141.8 x 22.1 x 11.6 feet built by J. Elder & Co. of Glasgow in 1881. Other yachts seen over the years at Plas Newydd were the *Princess Augusta, Liberty* and *Manna Lou*. Lord Anglesey, writing to Plas Newydd on 31 July 1909 while visiting Cowes, Isle of Wight on board the SY *Zaza*, stated that the use of a buoy would be preferable to anchoring:

> … I want one to belong permanently to me and to have Plas Newydd painted on it … with a strength to hold 1,000 ton boat … the boat I have now is about 500 tons … . [PN 5854]

Due to shortages during the First World War, a letter dated 13 October 1917, from the Ministry of Munitions Central Stores Branch in London and addressed to Captain Evans, 2 Bridge Street, Menai Bridge, referred to:

> … Lead Ballast ex. Yacht *Flirt* Owner Marquess of Anglesey 13 October 1917: Ministry of Munitions Defence of the Realm Act 1914 Hereby takes possession of all lead forming the inside ballast of the yacht *Flirt* now situate at Menai Straits. Payment made of £26 per ton net with the Ministry paying the cost of the removal of the lead … [PN5859]

In the inter-war period, the Marquess of Anglesey owned the *Alert*, of 147 tons and measuring 103' 8" x 23' 6" x 11' 1" a three-masted schooner which had been built in Runcorn by Brundrit & Co in 1885. She had a crew of four and originally carried cod from Newfoundland to Europe but, when this trade ended, she then carried coal from north-east Wales to Cornwall, returning with a load of china clay for use in the potteries. Salt, used in the

The Alert *moored alongside the Caernarfon slate quay. [Author]*

preservation of fish during its voyages across the Atlantic, had impregnated the woodwork of the ship's hold to such an extent, that it could be tasted by running a finger against the wood.

After a period of being laid up at Runcorn, the *Alert* was bought by the Marquess of Anglesey and towed to Plas Newydd by the SS *Enid*, one of the Dinorwic Quarry ships, with Captain Hugh David Parry in command. Also on board the *Enid* was Captain Thomas Lillie, who would eventually take charge of the *Alert*, and Eric Owen, his assistant. As a result of the tow-rope parting outside Rhyl, a jib sail was raised on the *Alert* which allowed her to proceed, with no further assistance from the *Enid*, until they reached Puffin Island, where a new tow-rope was attached in order that she could be towed safely through the strait to Plas Newydd.

Whilst in the harbour at Plas Newydd, Watkin Jones, a local cabinet-maker, improved the vessel's saloon woodwork and living quarters. Before she could be authorised to carry passengers, a Board of Trade inspection and Lloyds survey had to be carried out and, for this purpose, she was towed to Port Dinorwic. As a result of this a number of defects were found and the ship was taken to Caernarfon for the masts to be lowered. It was eventually found that the cost of rectifying the problems would be prohibitive and she was towed back to Port Dinorwic, where she ended her days as a hulk on the foreshore and her woodwork being removed for a variety of uses.

Vaynol

Mr Thomas Assheton Smith (1776–1858) of Vaynol, whose land also extended down to the Menai Strait, had the benefit of a boathouse and small harbour within sight of Plas Newydd on the opposite side of the Menai Strait. Not only was Assheton Smith interested in sailing, he also had the ability to design steam vessels. *Menai*, the first to be built by Robert Napier at a cost of £20,000 and delivered to him at Bristol, had the benefit of three keels to prevent rolling. She was commanded by Captain Edwards, who was also involved with the *Matilda* [VP4430 & 4471]. Napier also built the following yachts for Assheton Smith:

YEAR BUILT	NAME	TONNAGE	HORSE POWER	BUILT OF
1830	*Menai*	400	120	wood
1838	*Glowworm*	300	100	iron
1840	*Fire-King*	700	230	wood
1844	1 *Fire-Queen*	110	30	iron
1845	2 *Fire-Queen*	230	80	iron
1846	3 *Fire-Queen*	300	120	iron
1849	*Jenny Lind*	220	70	iron
1851	*Sea Serpent*	250	80	iron

Prior to acquiring the *Pandora* (82897), G. W. D. Assheton Smith had the task of disposing of his steam yacht *Vaynol* (length 75') which he described as '… very pretty but rather expensive'. She was eventually sold for £650 in December 1869 [GAS, VP 2379/2700].

Pandora was a screw brig of 197 tons, length 146', breadth 25' and depth 12'. She was designed and built at HM Dockyard, Pembroke in 1867 as the gunboat *Newport*. When acquired from the Royal Navy in 1874 by Captain (later Sir) Allan Young, she was strengthened and fitted for Arctic navigation. It was for this reason that she was purchased by G. W. D. Assheton Smith, who shared a sense of adventure and a love of the sea with his predecessor Thomas Assheton Smith.

In preparation for the Arctic trip, and whilst on a visit to the Isle of Wight, work costing £262 3s. 9d. was carried out to the yacht's engine by H. Guy at the Solent Steam Engine & Boiler Works in May 1882 [GAS, VP 3107]. Other items listed were the purchase of shoes for the crew £20 3s., fishing lines £1 3s. 1d. and ammunition £152 17s. As an altruistic gesture, the wives of members of the crew were paid a weekly allowance whilst their husbands were at sea.

Amongst the guests on board the *Pandora* on the first Arctic voyage were William Lort, who acted as Assheton Smith's secretary and manager at Vaynol and his daughter Eurgain (known as Guiney) Beatrice who was to spend her sixteenth birthday on board on July 31 1882. During the two voyages made by the *Pandora* to the Arctic, the Lort diaries describe the apparent preoccupation Assheton Smith had with the collecting of animal and bird samples, a typical and unfortunate tendency during the Victorian era. Few details are given of the other guests on board. The papers disclose that other members of the crew were: Captain W. Preston, Sailing Master Jones, Chief Engineer J. Kingsworth, 2nd Engineer Owen Thomas and seaman Francis Jones [GAS, VP 4555].

After crossing the Arctic Circle on July 5 1882, and leaving Tromso four days later for Hammerfest some 130 miles away, they encountered the first hazard in the inhospitable waters, when they were suddenly enveloped in a mist. When it cleared, they found themselves solidly lodged in ice.

18 July: Soon after dinner a good deal of anxiety was felt as the incompetency [sic] of our ice pilot became more evident. We have still an interminable noisy barrage of ice roaring on our starboard quarter … Captain Preston acted with great promptitude & skill & I think did wonders in getting the ship out of the really perilous position she was in.

When they extricated the ship, they continued to Hammerfest and dropped anchor there about 11.30pm. Five days later on Sunday July 23:

We were within a cable length of where we were to anchor when the ship struck a rock & stuck bows on. Every effort was made to back her off but without success. This was a terrible disaster but the worst was to come. Mr Jones, sailing master, fell down & never recovered. He is to be buried close to where he ended his work in the pretty church, Kirkenes Island, Klosterely Fiord.

A report on the incident stated that '… the master (W. Preston) stated that the position of the rock was incorrectly laid down in the chart …'. A diver later checked her hull and she was certified as being seaworthy on the 6 September 1882.* [GAS, VP 4946]

26 July Wednesday: The Squire, Captain Preston, myself and nearly the whole ship's company left the ship for the pretty church on the island of Kirkenes to see our poor old sailing master Mr Jones put into his last home … The men sang some hymns — Welsh ones.

29 July Saturday: We were only 5 minutes behind time for dinner, after which Mr Assheton Smith, Guiney and I went ashore in the gig with the Rev. George Sandberg to take a last look at the grave of our old sailing master whose lot it is to rest so far from his kindred.

12 August Saturday: I rose with thoughts of home & grouse. We divided into three parties today. The Squire, Olsen, Kent & the dogs went one way. Guiney, I & Peter Monk the Dane, as one of the sailors informed the Squire at night,

* At the end of the voyage she was examined at Holyhead dry dock by Thomas Devonald of B & F Shipping, surveyor for the Lloyds Register, and it was recommended that she be repaired 'with similar material to the original'. The cost of repairs by William Williams of Holyhead amounted to £226 14s. and this was covered by the Commercial Union Assurance Company [GAS, VP , 4946].

'took our departure and steered north'. Captain Preston & Mr Williams the mate went another way.

15 August Tuesday: Captain P & my daughter shot on another island & their bag was 10 brace of ripar, 1 merganser & 1 diver. The name of the island is Noglan or Key Island … The waste & destruction of timber on some of the islands is lamentable. It reminds me of what was done in America when I was first there in 1841 & what must have been done by the Welsh who destroy but never replant.

17 August Thursday: The launch, the gig & the dinghy brought us all to Aaro. The Squire, seeing no chance to secure geese upon the water, landed Kent with a sailor & my 4 bore on the mainland to climb over to the osprey's nest then went off himself to try for an eagle.

18 August Friday: We dropped anchor at Tomoso at 2pm & heard that the Swedish Expedition had returned south a week ago. She had encountered much ice & had lost 2 men by accidents. Observed for the first time darkness in my stateroom.

28 August Monday: We left Surgaard, but not before Captain P & I had beaten some of the most beautiful & curious covert I ever saw for ripar. As usual, we saw little or nothing shootable on our way home to the ship. Weaver, the Squire's valet, who had got into a covert to beat for Captain P & me had a fit. We were all heartily glad to get on board the dear comfortable old ship after our long rough ride.

2 September Saturday: We were all wet through. The guns were constantly soaked with sea & rain; but thanks to their make Powell & Son they worked to perfection & did not give us the least trouble … The Northern Lights seen in perfection.

6 September Wednesday: An additional pilot took us into the river, where a diver examined the keel & pronounced us 'seaworthy'. In the afternoon I took Guiney on shore & showed her the Cathedral, which is undergoing repairs, and the other sights of the town.

7 September Thursday: We saw Sir H. Vivian & his nephew & Mr Pemberton sail for Halle in the old steamer *Tasso*. Ernest Vivian who came here from Stockholm & Germany in the morn: dined with us in the *Pandora*. Pemberton had been at Senja for nearly three months looking for bears which he did not find, albeit, I believe, he had good fishing & did not complain so much as I expected of mosquitoes.

10 September Sunday: This is said to be the country for the lynx. The Vice Consul at Trondheim, Herr Kjeldberg, told us that some children of Major Chadwick picked up & played with two young lynx kittens & eventually took them home. A man who chanced to pass this spot the next day was seriously mauled by the old lynx.

16 September Saturday: A brown she-bear was taken on board in the whaleboat. She soon hugged the carpenter & tore Peter's face & so Mr Assheton Smith decided, as she would not behave herself, to send her ashore.

20 September Wednesday: There was a concert at night in the saloon. Some of the music was of a high order. John Jones cockson (sic) of the gig gave us the 'Beggar Girl' in Welsh & I never was better pleased.

22 September Friday: Several Port Dinorwic vessels & two yachts seen. Went late into Oban. Letters were brought on board. The *Katherine* and other yachts here.*

Once again Lort continued with his diary of the 1884 cruise after some initial notes giving details of the family:

The Squire and owner of *Pandora* is George William Duff Assheton Smith, son of Robert Gordon Duff of Wellington Lodge, Ryde, IOW. He added Assheton Smith to his name upon inheriting Vaynol and the slate properties at age 11 in 1859, at which time the income was £40,000 per year. This amount increased substantially over the years. When he died in 1904, he was described as the richest commoner in the Kingdom. His brothers are Henry Assheton Duff and Charles Gordon Duff. Their sister Louise is married to Hussey Crespigney Vivian who they visit at Elsinore. He was envoy extraordinary and minister plenipotentiary to Denmark.

24 June Tuesday: At 9 o'clock on the morning of Tuesday the 24th June 1884, the grand old ship *Pandora* left her moorings opposite to the Vaynol boathouse in the Menai Straits & proceeded to sea midst great firing & cheering ashore & aboard. She crossed the Carnarvon bar, discharged her pilot & stood well off for the coast of Ireland. The Wexford hills were plainly seen before night.

26 June Thursday: … we betook ourselves to the Western Yacht Club to write letters & to partake of luncheon.

27 June Friday: After a lovely run we dropped anchor just opposite to Wellington Lodge, the residence of Mr Duff, he having met us in his yacht *Torfrida*.

28 June Saturday: We went on board the *Tofrida*, the most beautifully fitted up craft I ever saw, and then went ashore

* During the latter part of the 19th century a great number of expeditions sailed into the arctic region to seek 'a sea route to the North Pole'. A Mr Leigh Smith in his ship *Eira* was one such explorer but, it later transpired, his ship had hit a reef and sunk off Franz-Josef Land in October 1881 and for the next eight months, having rescued some supplies from the ship, he and his crew survived in a hut. Since nothing had been heard of Leigh Smith for over twelve months, Sir Allan Young (the previous owner of the *Pandora*) organised a Relief Expedition [Royal Geographical Society 1883 Report].

Left: William Lort. [Roma Lort Jones]
Above right: Beatrice Eurgain Hutton Lort.
[Roma Lort Jones]

to shop & to the Club. Mr Duff had luncheon on board the *Pandora*. At 6pm we sailed with a head wind & a favourable tide.

5 July Saturday: I have omitted to put in the programme of yesterday: our visit to the fine ship *Glanperis* of Carnarvon, bound for Sydney, and owned by the Squire's workmen; and the *Alice Platt* bound for Valpariso. I thought Captain Thomas, Master of the latter vessel, one of the most intelligent men I had met. Each ship was about a thousand tons & carried about 1600 tons. The *Glanperis* cost, when new, 6 years ago, £16,000 & the *Alice Platt* £17,000.

9 July Wednesday: At about 10am the Honourable C. Vivian came on board & we hauled out. He, having business in Copenhagen, is going there with us … Soon after leaving Elsinore we passed near the Swedish island of Ven, on which, Mr Vivian told me, one of the greatest astronomers of all time resided. The Hon. H. C. Vivian dined on board at night. Afterwards, we all went to the Tivoli Gardens & … tried a trip on the wonderful Russian Railway, quite a novel experience in the matter of travelling. Some of our party went in boats & balloons, all worked by steam.

12 July Saturday: One of the hands, Jack Hughes, injured his hand severely with a marlin spike. Mr White came on board, breakfasted with us & explained the dilemma he was in as to his getting to Kalmar. The Squire asked him to go with us & he soon had his things on board. The *Primrose* got off with us & we could see her astern for a long time.

13 July Sunday: At 2.30am I was disturbed by a terrible shock. I thought it was the repetition of an old experience, but no, it was a new one. We were in collision with the full-rigged brig *Baltic* of Rostock & a nice mess was made of both of us. Still, it might have been vastly worse. No lives were lost & only one man, the one on our forecastle upon the lookout, was injured at all. We stood by & eventually towed the brig into Karlskrona, there to await instructions from the underwriters. Herr Palander the Consul there came on board with the skipper of the brig. The latter tried hard to bring about an immediate settlement of his outrageous claim of £800.

23 July Wednesday: Captain P. had to go ashore for a pilot & so Mr Trollope, Mr Duff & I got up early & joined them. The launch *Carl* towed our gig … Brain the steward went into the market & bought good mutton at 40 ore & salmon at 60 ore per pound.

29 July Tuesday: As Captain Preston had to go to Umea in the steam launch for a bill of health, Mr Duff, Mr Trollope, Mr Vivian & I got up early & joined him. We had not got far when Roberts, one of the crew, called our attention to a stoat swimming across the river. The launch was stopped & I put in a cartridge & shot it.

3 August Sunday: Blayer, the head steward, went into some island & brought back a grebe & her young ones alive. The latter were very prettily striped with white upon a brown ground.

11 August Monday: We dropped anchor close to the Emperor's yacht, a splendid paddle wheel steamer: and not far from the *Czarina*, Mr Albert Brassey's yacht. Mr Duff, Mr Vivian & Mr Trollope left for St Petersburg. I went in the steam launch with Mr Assheton Smith to a landing where the boats were as thick as vehicles in The Strand.

12 August Tuesday: Mr Duff, Mr Trollope, Mr Vivian & Captain Preston came on board early. Mr Duff & I had a wet rough journey in the launch to meet the 3 o'clock boat for St Petersberg. The steam boat got in late & there were three steam launches at the pier waiting for arrivals by the boat. The *Emperor's* launch, the *Pandora's* launch & the *Czarina's* launch.

14 August Thursday: I got up early & went ashore in the steam launch with the mate. As I returned in the dinghy to the *Pandora*, a good three mile pull for Mahoney & Jack Hughes. I called on the *Czarina*, certainly a gentleman's yacht of the first class, but, after all, I should prefer to be in the *Pandora* in really bad weather.

19 August Tuesday: Mr Duff & Captain Preston came on board early in the afternoon & brought Mr Vivian's lovely children, George, Dorothy & Violet; and an invitation for me to dinner at 6.45. There were at the dinner the host & hostess, the Solicitor General & his young & interesting wife, Mr Duff, Miss Ellis – a nice well-informed lady, Mr Raikes, the Hon. C. Vivian's secretary, just 6ft 7inches, Captain Preston & myself.

25 August Monday: Towards night we anchored in Tobermory Bay, so as to have daylight for the navigation of the narrow passage of the Sound of Mull. Many large Yachts in the bay, one a beauty, the *Wanderer* belonging to Mr Lambert.

27 August Wednesday: I saw the Chicken Rock through the porthole as I was dressing, & the sea was like a mill pond & very unlike what it was on the night of our return from the Arctic Regions in 1882. A little haze kept us from going so fast as we might. But in due course Point Lynas Lighthouse was a welcome object on our starboard bow & the well-known pilot came on board & soon told us we were too late for the tide in the Swillies & so we anchored off Beaumaris where there was goodly gathering of yachts, some to contend in the races of the morrow & some to dispense hospitalities & to be admired.

On the 1 December 1884, following her return from the Arctic, repairs were carried out to the *Pandora's* engine by De Winton & Co. of Caernarfon* [GAS, VP 2379, pp351] .

As the result of George Duff Assheton Smith dying without a son, the Vaynol estate was inherited by his brother, Charles, who did not share his enthusiasm for wild animals. He did enjoy sailing the SY *Amathea* to the south of France and Italy. When not touring abroad, the yacht was often to be seen moored on the Strait or tied up in the dock at Port Dinorwic in the early years of the twentieth century.

The SY *Amalthea*, described as a twin-masted iron screw schooner of 204 tons and measuring 189.3 x 27.1 x 15.0 feet, was built by Ramage & Ferguson at Leith in 1881 for T. J. Waller and registered in London under the name of *Iolanthe*. She was purchased by A. Mortimer Singer of New York in 1889 and, three years later by Sir Donald Currie, KCMG, MP who sold her to the Duke of Montrose in 1899 who renamed her *Mione*. When she was purchased by James Horlick in 1902, the name reverted to *Iolanthe*. Her name remained the same when she was purchased by Mrs F. Calvert in 1906 but, in 1907 when she was purchased by Charles Garden Assheton Smith of Vaynol, he changed her name to *Amalthea*. Whilst in his possession, certain design changes were carried out to the stern and promenade deck by Cox & Kings, Naval Architects of London and, at the same time, a new smoking room was added. Her engine consisted of three furnaces which produced a working pressure of 80lbs [DQ 3008, 3467, 3480]. There are no records of any pleasure cruises that she may have been used for and, twelve months after Assheton Smith's death in 1914, she was requisitioned by the Admiralty. Nothing is known of her movements until the autumn of 1918, when she was being used at the naval base HMS *Iolaire* at Stornoway, where for ease of identification her name was changed to *Iolaire*.

Following the end of the First World War in November 1918, men from the Isle of Lewis, many who had been away in the services since the beginning of the conflict, were anxious to get home so as to be with their families and to celebrate Hogmanay. Arrangements had been made for the men to travel by train, initially to Inverness

---

* William Lort, FRCS, formerly of Fron Goch Hall, Llanllugan, Montgomeryshire, died at Vaynol Old Hall 23 May 1891 age 69. He was described as a 'Great Traveller and Explorer and Noted Judge of Animals'. His daughter, Eurgain Beatrice Lort Stancliffe died 12 July 1950 age 83 and both are buried at Llanfairisgaer cemetery, Felinheli.

Above: Larboard view of the Amalthea *at anchor on the Menai Strait.* [Gareth Jones]

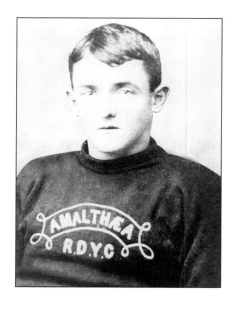

Centre left: Amalthea *in dock at Port Dinorwic.* [Author]

Centre right: A member of the Amalthea *crew.* [Port Dinorwic Historical Society]

Left: The starboard view of the Amalthea *at anchor on the Menai Strait.* [Vernon Bowles]

Steam tender from the SY Amalthea *in Port Dinorwic.*
[Port Dinorwic Historical Society]

and then to Kyle where they would, or should, be able to catch a boat home to Lewis. The normal ferry, the SS *Sheila* (belonging to MacBrayne Shipping Company) was unable to cope with the additional passengers and HMS *Iolaire* (previously the *Amalthea*) was sent from Stornoway to assist, despite the fact that her normal crew complement was reduced by half due to Christmas leave. Nevertheless, that still left a crew of twenty-one together with the Captain, 1st Officer and Chief Engineer.

When the *Iolaire* cast off at 19.30 hours on New Years Eve she was carrying 190 servicemen (this figure, supposedly the number of men that were counted on to the boat, is at variance with that quoted at the two inquiries) although she only carried 80 life-jackets and lifeboats for 100 men. The weather forecast was for a reasonable trip, but by 00.30 hours the wind was freshening and the *Iolaire* encountered squalls and drizzling rain. In Stornoway harbour, HM Drifter *Budding Rose* was waiting for the *Iolaire* and to act as her pilot-boat but, as a result of seeing a rocket fired at about 01.55 hours, her captain went to investigate and found a vessel in distress. Sadly, no assistance could be provided as the *Iolaire* was on the rocks and there were heavy seas running. According to subsequent inquiry reports, the *Iolaire* had missed the harbour entrance in the darkness even though lights were being shown. A Naval Inquiry held on 8 January, and a Public Inquiry on 10 February 1919, revealed that of the 284 men on board the *Iolaire* there had been only 79 survivors.

Port Dinorwic Sailing Club — the early days

Yacht racing along the Menai Strait has been a popular pastime over many years, but the craft, usually of ten tons and more, that made spectacular and no doubt enjoyable sailing, were mostly owned by landowners and wealthy families. Yachts such as the *Mayflower* (24-tons), *Almida* (24-tons), *Molita* (19-tons) and *Wallaroo* (25-tons) that competed in the latter part of the nineteenth century, usually carried

Some idea of the size of the 637-ton SY Amalthea *can be gained from this photograph showing Thomas Griffith standing in the dry-dock alongside the rudder and propeller .*
[Author]

a crew of five or more, composed of local men who had the necessary expertise and knowledge of the Strait's idiosyncrasies. According to a private record, kept by John Roberts, an Assistant Harbour Master at Holyhead, he and Captain Skinner went out into the bay to 'consider and recommend the best route for sailing on Regatta Day 17 July 1855 which was experiencing a brisk breeze from the west but clear weather'. *Glance* won the first race, *Surprise* the second and the third was won by the *Gibsy*. The observation was made that 'many strangers were in town on the occasion' [UCNW, MS 25773]. Regattas being held at Beaumaris, Caernarfon and Llandudno were reported in local papers in 1874. Even though a similar event was held at Port Dinorwic in 1888, at the time when Captain Bennett (commander of Assheton Smith's SS *Pandora*) was chairman of the Regatta Committee, it did not appear in the local press.

Whilst the yachts were racing, the spectators on the shore would be entertained by one of the local bands such as the *Clio* Fife and Drum or the Port Dinorwic Brass Band conducted by Patrick Ayres. George Edward Griffiths (1827–1901), who had been very much involved with yachting and local regattas, had a memorial erected in his memory by the Port Dinorwic Regatta Committee 'to mark their appreciation of his public spirit'.

The master mariners, who had served the greater part of their lives aboard sailing-ships and who had 'come ashore' to retire, would keep their hand in by sailing small dinghies sporting a burgee consisting of a white cross on a blue background and the initials PDYC thereon. Other retired mariners, perhaps adopting a more sedentary approach, sailed model yachts on the Strait. The old quay barracks, now long gone, was used as the first clubhouse or 'headquarters'.

Yachting and boating on the Strait was very much curtailed during the Second World War, to the extent that all boat owners had to have a permit. A letter written June 1942 stated that:

> Fishing and pleasure boat activities severely restricted. Jones is very fond of yachting. As this is prohibited at the moment he has converted his craft into a fishing boat. Capt. Thomas does not believe that Jones does any fishing but pretends to do so, so as to obtain a licence … to take his boat out [XD15 30/95].

PORTDINORWIC MODEL YACHT CLUB.

COMMITTEE:

Commodore:
CAPT. BEN WILLIAMS.

Vice-Commodore:
CAPT. T. LILLIE.

Chairman:
MR W. H. WILLIAMS, Moranedd.

Treasurer:
MR. T. P. OWEN.

Secretary:
MR JOHN WILLIAMS, Belmont.

MR. ARTHUR ROBERTS, MR. H. W. SIMPSON, MR. S. CHUBB, and MR. ROWLAND WILLIAMS.

Left: Port Dinorwic Model Yacht Club membership card, c.1900. [Margaret Tuzuner]

Below: Five retired mariners with one of their model yachts. [Emyr Wyn Roberts]

The following permits were issued as 'Rowboat Rosters' 30 September 1942:

John Jones, 1 Rhyd Fenai, Bush Road	*Lark*	16'	M102
Morris Thomas, 10 Beach Road	*Tom*	10'	M114
T Preston, Tynewydd	*Dot*	13'	M116
William Owen, 4 Jubilee Terrace	*Jet*		M120
Roberts & Sons	*Pip*	10'	M123
J. Smallwood, Gwaithdy	*Squib*	12'	M125
J. Tildsley, Bryn Melyn	*Betty*	13'	M129
Mr A. E. Williams, Westfields	*Pip*		M133
W. J. Parry, 24 Seaview Terrace	*Jean & Nigger*		M138
J. E. Parker, Old Shipyard	*Pram*	10'	M141
Col. R. R. Davies, Min y Garth, Glyn Garth	*Anne*	14'	M142
O. T. Williams, Plas Dinorwic	*Wren*	10'	M152
R. J. Bowles, 18 Beach Road	*Leslie*	12'	M153

Sailing and participation in regattas was at one time, the prerogative of the rich, albeit that they relied on the not-so-rich to sail or crew the vessels for them. Gradually, the pattern changed over the years, especially in the second half of the twentieth century, with yachting becoming very popular more especially since there was a huge variety of craft available.

After the restrictions imposed by the Second World War, people were keen to renew their interest in sailing and to actually participate rather than adopt the passive role of previous years. Since most families in the village had one or more relatives connected with the sea, it was inevitable that there would be tremendous interest in sailing. When affordable yachts became available directly after the war, it provided a greater opportunity for more to participate. Youngsters were taught from an early age how to handle a sailing-craft until it became second-nature.

At the inaugural meeting held on 23 June 1947, at the Memorial Hall for 'Yacht and Boat owners and others interested', it was decided that a sailing club would be formed and that its members would agree to race under the Yacht Club Association (YCA) rules. Such an arrangement would then allow the club to compete against other yacht clubs. The twenty-three men who attended (all but one lived at Port Dinorwic) agreed 'that a Club be formed … and that it would be called The Port Dinorwic Sailing Club'. Membership fee was set at 5s. (25p). Mr R. W. Roberts agreed to record the minutes of the meeting and act as secretary, provided 'the Sailing Club does not countenance nor sanction Sunday racing under auspices of the Club'. The other officials elected were Commodore — Mr O. T. Williams (General Manager of the Dinorwic Quarry); Vice Commodore — Llewelyn Jones; Chairman — Mr John Roberts; Treasurer — A. E. Williams. Others involved in the initial meeting were: Mrs O. G. Roberts, Messrs Bob Bowles, R. R. Evans, John G. Jones, J. P. Jones, Jack T. Jones, L. Lloyd Jones, R. H. Jones, L. Morgan, William Owen, John Parry, H. Pennington, J. Preece, E. O. Roberts, Titus Roberts, W. E. Roberts, Y. G. Smith, Alf Thomas, Morris Thomas, David Thomas, T. H. Williams and J. C. Wilson.

When the first official race of the 'new' sailing club took place 7 July 1947 at Corbetts Bay, the officials had the benefit of a table and two chairs borrowed from a nearby house. For time-keeping, they used a 'station clock' and

Port Dinorwic, Regatta Morn. 1905   J. S. Thomas, Chemist.

Left: Port Dinorwic Regatta, 1905.
[Port Dinorwic Historical Society]

Below: Port Dinorwic Yacht, 1930s.
[Emyr Wyn Roberts]

races were started with the aid of a shotgun, whose owner sometimes ran out of blank cartridges. If this happened, then he resorted to using live ones which produced either a shower of shot pellets over the racing yachts, or shredded the signal flags, depending on the trajectory of the gun and the mood of the starter.

Amongst the 'nondescript' boats taking part during this period were: *Firecrest, Jewel, Breezy Ann, Atomic, Thunderbolt* (an old square stern ship's lifeboat converted to a sailing-boat), *Skeed, Slip, Red Diver* and *Jina*. In the post-war years, because material of every description was in short supply, some of the yachts resorted to making sails out of old flour bags — Rigby, Frost or National Flour. Such material had the disadvantage of stretching, when subjected to wet weather, also spectators were aware of the type of flour bag being used since the name could not be obliterated.

In July 1947, it was decided that the 'new' Club Burgee would be changed to a red dragon on a green background with the letters PDSC but, at a later meeting, the momentous decision was taken that it would be in the form of the dragon rampant (rearing or standing in profile on the left hind-leg) instead of a dragon passant (walking and looking to dexter [right] side with three paws on the ground and forepaw raised).

With an increasing club membership came the need for a clubhouse. Having inspected various structures at RAF Valley, it was eventually decided to purchase a hut for £75, which was erected by the firm of Dowsett Mackay which had been involved in the construction of landing barges at Dinas during the war.

At the first meeting in the 'new' clubhouse (which consisted of the main hall, kitchen and committee room) held on 3 August 1948, their assets were listed as three cups, one stop-watch, three-dozen playing cards, one bell on stand, one gavel, land secured on tenancy of 2 shillings per annum and a registered burgee.

The Clubhouse was opened by Sir Michael Duff on 16 November 1948, and shortly afterwards, enquiries were

Port Dinorwic Regatta programme, 1931.
[Gwynedd Archives Service]

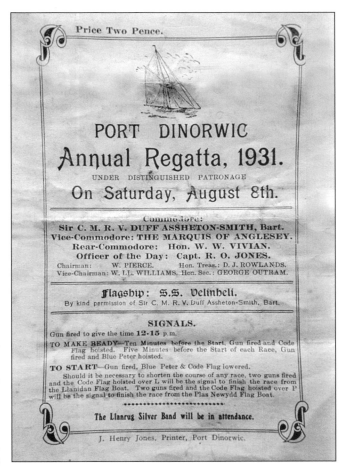

being made regarding the holding of functions in the building. It was decided that the playing of games such as darts, draughts, dominoes and cards be allowed in the clubhouse, but 'any member found guilty of gambling be expelled'. The contentious matter of the club applying for a 'licence to sell intoxicating drinks' was raised from time to time, but a meeting held 18 March 1948 resolved not to apply for a liquor licence.

A meeting of the sailing committee and prospective purchasers of new boats met at the office of Roberts & Sons on 10 February 1948, to discuss the Brooke Marine new design 16-foot boat which could be purchased at a cost of £300 'with full specification'. It was decided that the price was much too high and the secretary was asked to write to the Yacht Racing Association for its assistance in locating second-hand boats 'somewhere in the region of £150 each, about seven in number and of strictly the same size'. On 24 February, an offer was received from P. Waters & Son, Appledore, Devon to supply three boats, to be known as the Port Dinorwic One-Design (PDOD), at a price of £130 18s. 10d. plus carriage of £9 16s. 5d. making a total of £140 15s. 3d. each.

The first 16-foot Port Dinorwic One-design yacht to arrive in the village was the boat to be named *Fulmar*. This was clinker-built with bowsprit and gunter rig and a heavy steel centre plate. With its small jib, large main and overhanging boom and no cleats, it was quite a handful to sail in any breeze, especially on the run. It had been originally designed in 1905 by I. S. Marriott and built by P. Waters for the Taw and Torridge Sailing Club.

Inevitably, because of the variations in design between the boats, caused by the builders not having a uniform plan to work from, attempts were made by the sailing committee to have a standard design based on the original boat, namely *Fulmar*. The next stage in standardisation occurred when a new yacht arrived in 1950, purchased by Dr Henry Edwards. The initial reaction was that she should be banned from racing against the One-Design because of the differences in deck design, rig and boom. However, when a trial race was arranged with Eric Owen at the helm against the established PDOD, the new boat won easily. On the strength of such a performance, it was decided that the sails, booms and gaffs of the other PDOD would be suitably modified, so as to equate with Dr Edwards' new boat so producing some semblance of uniformity. However, the inevitable variations in the boats, whether by design or later adaptation by the owners, produced a variety of unexpected results in performance which were not always to the benefit of the crew. The lack of consistency in the performance of the different boats was attributed to the variations in the design. One boat would have a heavier centre plate (*Fulmar*) and, consequently, perform well in heavy weather, as compared to another (*Patsy*) which was a much lighter boat and did well when a light wind blew. However, since *Gypsy* per-formed well in most conditions, it soon became

Top left: Port Dinorwic Sailing Club Racing at Beaumaris, 1950. [*Author*]

Top right: Port Dinorwic Sailing Club racing at Bangor, 1950 (J63 'Jewel' class of Rhyl). [*Author*]

Centre left & right: Port Dinorwic Sailing Club 'One-design' boats. [*Alun Lewis Jones*]

Left: Regatta at Port Dinorwic. The Seiont II is being used as the flagship. [*Emyr Wyn Roberts*]

apparent that it was due to Eric Owen's skill as helms-man.

The names applied to the Port Dinorwic One-Design yachts (or PD 16-footers as they became known) and their original owners were:

1. *Ellen*	John Maguire		5. *Gypsy*	Dr Elwyn Rowlands
2. *Wyn*	Roberts & Son		6. *Barbette*	Royal Artillery, Tŷ Croes
3. *Julia*	Alec Dancer		7. *Yimkin*	Ewart Davies
4. *Fulmar*	David Lloyd		8. *Thesia*	Dr Henry Edwards

Rather than have their yachts identified from the shore from a number on the sail, some of the owners brought individuality by introducing coloured sails, e.g. *Fulmar* — green; *Gypsy* — blue; *Patsy* — red and *Thesia* — yellow. It was not unknown for one or two to dye the sails red, by soaking them in cochineal in a large bath and then hanging them up to dry. However, as soon as they were subjected to wet conditions the dye ran on to the crew.

The crew's dress could also be as varied as the colour of the sails. One individual invited to experience the art of sailing, turned up wearing a Gannex raincoat and brogue shoes. In the early days of sailing, until the 'correct style' had been adopted, a trilby hat was quite normal. One crew member, supposedly well versed in all maritime matters, would find that his pullover would be three times its original length after being subjected to a thoroughly wet trip. Another individual who had a similar experience, was the local Calvinistic Methodist minister who was being taken for a sail on *Wyn* but, whilst in the course of boarding the vessel at Dinas, when he had one foot on a ladder and the other on the boat, the inevitable happened. Rumours circulating through the village suggested that he had left his own sect and joined the Baptists!

With an increasing number of yachts and races came the question of safety. Initially, the sailing committee felt that it would be sufficient that 'each boat must carry lifebelts or life-jackets in an accessible place, for each person on board' but a further decision taken in March 1948, stated that the wearing of life-savers be compulsory. Within four years, races were being held on Wednesday evenings as well as Saturday afternoons between May and September. With an increasing number of boats participating in the races by 1952, it was agreed that the remaining monies held in the Jetty Fund would be used to purchase a rescue boat — *Pat II*. When she developed a leak and liable to be out of commission at a time of emergency a Dell Quay dory was purchased at a cost of £300.

Port Dinorwic Regatta officials on the bridge of the SS Velinheli, *1938.*
[Maragaret Tuzuner]

Left: SS Enid as flagship during the Port Dinorwic Regatta. [Emyr Wyn Roberts]

Below: Port Dinorwic Regatta, 1900. [Author]

From very parochial and humble beginnings, the Port Dinorwic Sailing Club has inevitably become more sophisticated. The original ex-RAF hut has long gone but, nevertheless, in the early years of the club, the facilities which it provided on a year-round basis, gave members a great deal of pleasure, as of course, did sailing those early yachts.

Local Characters

Amongst the numerous characters that lived in the village of Port Dinorwic, especially during the first half of the twentieth century, and who were involved in the early days of sailing on the Strait, or were closely associated with maritime matters, were Thomas Lillie, Titus Roberts and W. E. Parker.

Thomas Lillie (1866–1949)

According to Thomas Lillie's obituary, he was born in New Zealand in 1866, but census returns for the turn of the century state that his birthplace was Bristol. When he married Jane Jones in St. David's Church, Liverpool on 22 January 1889, his profession was given as sailor and his address as 15 Virginia Street, Liverpool. That same year they came to live at 7 Beach Road, Port Dinorwic where they had a son, Thomas John Lillie, born on 12 November 1889. His wife died on 3 December, aged 26. Thomas married for a second time, on 9 November 1896 at Hill Street Chapel, Wrexham, to Mary Jones. They had two daughters, Laura (born 16 June 1901) and Ada (born 22 September 1905) while they were living at 50 Bangor Street, Port Dinorwic.

From the time when he first came to live in the village in 1889, he crewed small coasters such as the schooner *Sarah* and the ketch *James* which was owned by Harry Jones Roberts. When he bought the *James* for £300 in 1910 he promoted himself to the rank of captain and, from that time on, he was always known as 'Captain Lillie'. Ten

Port Dinorwic Sailing Club Presentation Dinner, 1952. [Author]

years later he leased the ferry boat *Menai*, built by Crossfields at Conwy, the first of the ferry boats to be motorised. He operated this vessel successfully between Port Dinorwic and Moel y Don from 1920 to 1935. At the same time, he was also working at Plas Newydd as captain of the *Mauna Law* and *Lilly of Laguna*, both owned by Lord Anglesey. The latter vessel was sold by Lord Anglesey to Assheton Smith of Vaynol who, in turn, sold it Captain Lillie. He in turn sold it to Lord Newborough. When Lord Anglesey acquired the schooner *Alert*, it was Captain Lillie's responsibility to look after the vessel. He was also a keen member of both the Port Dinorwic Model Yacht Club and the Port Dinorwic Sailing Club.

His son, Thomas John Lillie, started his working career in January 1905, at the age of 15, as a stoker on one of the steam locomotives at the Dinorwic Quarry, but left after a few years to join his father as a member of the crew of the *Sarah*. When Thomas John Lillie was married on 3 April 1915, to Sarah Williams of 43 Crown Street, Caernarfon, at the Register Office, Liverpool, his marriage certificate stated that his occupation and address was 'saloon deck man' on the SS *Graphic*, Princes Dock, Liverpool. Following the death of his wife, T. J. Lilley married Winifred Eve Hocking of Church St., Newlyn, in September 1930 at the Parish Church of St. Paul, Penzance. He was involved with maritime matters at Penzance, until his death at the age of 45 from tuberculosis at the Tehidy Sanatorium, Camborne on 13 January 1937.

Mary and Thomas Lillie, died within a week of each other in 1949 and are buried at Llanfairisgaer.

Captain Thomas Lillie.
[Port Dinorwic Historical Society]

William Eaton Parker (1870–1951)

One man who appreciated the Menai Strait, and the beauty of the area as much as anyone, was William Eaton Parker. Born at Huyton Hall, Liverpool in 1870, the son of wealthy parents, Mr Parker had a great love for the water and, in particular, the Menai Strait and decided to build a house on land which he bought at Dinas, Felinheli in November 1909, the address of which was the Old Shipyard. He would emphasise his many maritime connections by having on his writing paper, reference to agencies such as 'The American Company's Marine Motors' and the 'Caille Perfection Two-Stroke Marine Engine'. He imported small boats (described locally as 'banana boats' because of their shape) but his own participation on water was limited to canal trips, which would entail taking his boat from Dinas by horse and cart to the local station, where it would be lifted on to a wagon for transporting to the Llangollen Canal at Chirk.

While waiting for the house to be built at Dinas, he and his wife lived in the old boat-building shed alongside the slipway and Mrs Parker, writing in 1909, described the sad state of the old ship-building yard:

… there are 2 or 3 sheds that have absolutely gone beyond repair — one is a mere skeleton. The place is altogether very untidy and would look better if clear of debris … office, ship carpenter's shed and loft and Dwelling House, sawpit and boat shed. Building not safe — props rotten.

William Eaton Parker died on 19 January 1951 at the age of 81 and his wife Alice Hilder Parker on 19 April 1968 at the age of 90. Their grave at Llanfairisgaer cemetery is as near as they can possibly be to the Strait, the stretch of water which they both loved.

Titus Roberts (1878–1954)

Another person who had close association with the Port Dinorwic Sailing Club in its early days, but in a non-participatory role, was Titus Roberts, who was born at 16 Berllan Bach, Bangor, on 10 August 1878. Married to Mary Jane Roberts in 1901, he spent most of his working life as a signalman on the railway. His initial venture was to purchase a boat called *Elvira*, powered by an army tank engine which ran on paraffin, and was steered with the aid of a car steering wheel. Such was the power of the engine when the throttle was opened, that the stern would tend to gradually to sink. His next venture, was to buy an old square stern ship's lifeboat, which had been converted to a sailing-boat by adding sails made by him out of old flour bags. Unfortunately, parts of the hull were not in a good state of repair, which caused his crew to spend most of the time bailing out water rather than concentrating on sailing. Following this, he bought two yachts which he named *Atomic* and the *Thunderbolt*. Although he personally never undertook the task of 'sailing' any of his boats, he would take great delight in seeing them being ably handled by local lads, such as Eric Owen and John McGuire. Titus Roberts died on 17 April 1954 aged 75.

Sailing: Liverpool to the Menai Strait

From the early part of the nineteenth century, travel by ship was a very popular pastime. For those who lived in the north-west of England, there were plenty of opportunities of boarding a ship at Liverpool during the summer months and sailing to Llandudno, Menai Bridge, Caernarfon and round Anglesey, before returning home. J. Hemmingway, writing in 1835, described a voyage from Liverpool to Menai Bridge and how much the passengers enjoyed the sea air:

> When the traveller who has visited Liverpool for the ulterior purpose of proceeding by water to Beaumaris, Bangor or Caernarvon, has satisfied his curiosity by a survey of the various objects which that town affords he will, every morning, find a fine steamer moored at the Pier Head, ready to receive and waft him across the waters from the shores of the Mersey to the straits of the Menai. The packets employed on this station are strong vessels admirably fitted up and manned with the choicest seamen; they are amply furnished with provisions and refreshments suitable for every grade of passenger and the utmost politeness and civility are enjoined upon both officers and the ship's company … a number of musicians constantly occupy the deck who entertain the company. Spacious and convenient docks shewing their forests of masts-piers and quays covered with people waiting for embarkation...towering warehouses towering in all the pride of commerce … the many steam vessels majestically wending their way. On the passage down the Mersey to the bosom of old ocean, the scenery on both sides the river, the Rock Perch, the rocks and caverns called the Red Noses, the several light-houses, the vessels approaching or departing or gliding on the horizon, the floating-light, the Welsh mountains and the river deep green colour of the sea, each become successively the topics of observation and the sources of pleasure. On rounding the Rock … the steamer passes a strong fort erected here a few years ago at the expense of Government … to protect the port … Arrived opposite the town of Beaumaris, the packet is stopped for a few minutes to give time for the landing of such of the passengers as have reached their intended destination; when the vessel proceeds onwards first to Garth Ferry where the passengers for Bangor are disembarked and then on to the Suspension Bridge.

Sailings from Liverpool to north Wales in 1936, for example, ran for Easter weekend and then for the period between 23 May and 21 September. The steamers *St. Tudno* or *St. Seiriol* left Liverpool at 10.45am and would be due to arrive at Llandudno, depending on weather conditions, at 1.05pm followed by Menai Bridge at 2.30pm. This would allow passengers just over an hour ashore, before catching the 3.45pm boat back to Llandudno. Passengers could also enjoy morning, afternoon and evening 'Sea Cruises', as well as occasional day trips to

SS St Elvis, *built by Fairfields at Gowan, passing the* Clio *moored off Bangor pier. Of 566 tons and capable of carrying 1,000 passengers at 18½ knots, she was in service until 1930.* [Author]

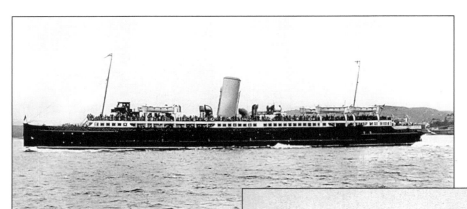

SS St Tudno on the Menai Strait. [Author]

SS La Marguerite on the Menai Strait. Built by Fairchild Shipbuilding and Engineering Co. Ltd., Glasgow, she carried many innovations such as 'lighted with electricity throughout' and 'equipped with Marconi Wireless Station'. She remained in service until 22 October 1925 when she was sold for scrap. [Author]

Above: SS Snowdon at Caernarfon landing stage, c.1910. She was built by Laird Bros. of Birkenhead in 1892 for the Snowdon Passenger Steam Ship Co. Ltd., of Liverpool. She was capable of carrying 462 passengers at a speed of 14 knots. After service as a minesweeper during the Great War she continued in service until 1931. The paddle-steamer passing at speed is the SS St Trillo heading for Menai Bridge. [Author]

SS Snowdon on the Menai Strait. [Emyr Wyn Roberts]

SS Bonnie Princess *off Beaumaris. [Author]*

Caernarvon from Llandudno by a new motor vessel *St. Silio*. Other vessels involved in these cruises, were the *La Marguerite*, the *St. Elvis* and the *Snowdon*, operated by the Liverpool & North Wales Steamship Company Limited of Liverpool.

The *St. Seiriol's* captain was Captain Robert Dop, a native of Port Dinorwic, who had been appointed master of the vessel in 1933. He was in command when the *St. Seiriol* had the distinction of being the first ship to be involved in the embarking of troops from the Dunkirk beaches during the war. In recognition of the bravery displayed by Captain Dop and his crew, a plaque, presented by Ronal Gross, the Minister of Shipping, was placed near the entrance of the *St. Seiriol's* saloon. It stated:

Captain Robert Dop of the TS St Seiriol. *[Port Dinorwic Historical Society]*

> Captain R. Dobb, [sic] Master of the *St Seiriol*, 17 June 1940.
> I write on behalf of the Government to convey to you and to members of your ship's company, the gratitude and admiration felt for the help freely given and the courage and endurance displayed by you all in the evacuation from Dunkirk. This operation, in which the Merchant Navy joined as partner of the fighting services, was carried to a successful conclusion in the face of difficulties never before experienced in war. I am proud to pay tribute to your share, and that of your ship's company, in a great and humane adventure destined to occupy a place of honour in the pages of history.

When that arduous and dangerous task was completed, the *St. Seiriol*, as part of her war-time rôle, transported troops on the Clyde and to Northern Ireland. When she resumed her peace-time rôle in Easter 1946, Captain Dop still had four members of the crew who were with him at Dunkirk, namely: Second

TS St Seiriol. [Author]

Engineer T. Bowler, Chief Steward J. Brown and two ABs J. Thomas and Ffrancon Roberts of Port Dinorwic. Captain Dop subsequently took over command of the *St. Tudno* in 1949. When he retired at the age of 64 in 1960, he had served the company for 40 years.

The plaque exhibited in the Saloon of the St Seiriol, *which was presented to the ship's crew by the Minister of Shipping in recognition of their service during the Dunkirk evacuation of 1940. [Author]*

8. Life-saving

The navigational aids available on modern ships, are in complete contrast to the few instruments available to the crews of sailing-ships. Irrespective of their size, these vessels would be very vulnerable to the weather and, since they lacked the manoeuvrability and speed of modern ships, there was little, if anything, that they could do to counteract the effects of a storm at sea. Losses amongst such ships, due to adverse weather, were frequent; the saving of lives was infrequent. In the days before radio became available for communication, in particular for transmitting distress calls, the loss of a ship would only be realised when it failed to return to its home port, after a certain length of time at sea or if the disaster had been witnessed by another vessel.

In an attempt to alleviate some of the dangers that ships could encounter along the Anglesey and Caernarfonshire coastlines, especially during the hours of darkness, a meeting held at the Guild Hall, Caernarfon on 23 October 1819, with Viscount Warren Bulkeley in the chair, decided that a lighthouse would be built on Bardsey Island and that ships in the vicinity would be charged a toll of 1 farthing (a quarter of an old penny) per ton of cargo carried. The light, which was seen for the first time on Christmas Eve 1821, is 140 feet above sea level.

Vessels entering the Menai Strait from the Abermenai end, had the benefit of a fixed-light tower built on Llanddwyn Island in 1846 by the Caernarvon Harbour Trust. In addition, a pilot (earning £10 per annum in 1938–9) who lived in a nearby cottage, would be available to assist vessels entering the Strait. Llanddwyn also had a lifeboat station, but this facility was withdrawn by the Royal National Lifeboat Institution (RNLI) in 1907 after having been in service for 76 years.

Prior to the founding of the RNLI in 1824, life-saving at sea would be dependent on the availability of privately funded lifeboats. The first to be built, in 1789, at South Shields, was followed by a number of locally organised craft around the coast of the United Kingdom. The aim of Sir William Hillary, who was responsible for establishing the RNLI, was to have lifeboat stations around the coast and for each one to be funded by a team of volunteers.

Following a local meeting held on 22 November 1828, '… to establish a Society … for the 'Preservation of Life from Shipwreck on the principle of the Royal National Institution" a letter was sent to the Marquess of Anglesey 'I am desired … to request your Lordship's sentiments on the subject and whether it would be most advisable to have it in connection with or independent of the Royal National Institution. [signed] John Williams' [UCNW, PN 1753]. The Marquess agreed to the formation of the 'Anglesey Local Association for the Preservation of Life from Shipwreck' and amongst its subscribers, was Thomas Assheton Smith of Vaenol who gave £5 in August 1828 [VP 4057]. As a result of this Association being formed, lifeboat stations were established at Moelfre (1830), Cemlyn, Holyhead, Beaumaris, Rhoscolyn, Penmon (1832) and Llanddwyn (1840). Subsequent to the Association amalgamating with the Royal National Lifeboat Institution in 1852, a further five stations were established on Anglesey before the end of the century. All of the stations mentioned have subsequently been closed, with the exception of Moelfre and Holyhead, which are today equipped with both conventional and inflatable inshore

Above: Launching the Llanddwyn lifeboat Richard Henry Gould *in 1906. The station was closed the following year. [Author]*

Below: Cottages on Llanddwyn island which housed the lifeboat crew, lighthouse keeper and the crews of pilot boats. [Author]

Above: Llanddwyn lighthouse, built in 1846 it remained in use until 1975. [Author]

lifeboats. Even though the lifeboat station at Beaumaris was closed in 1991, service continued to be provided with its inflatable inshore boat, which had been introduced in 1963. A similar inshore lifeboat station at Trearddur Bay was established in 1967. In addition, Porthdinllaen covers the area around Lleyn and the approaches to the Menai Strait.

Porthdinllaen Lifeboat

Station History:

1864 — A lifeboat house constructed at a cost of £140.

1888 — A new lifeboat house and slipway constructed at a cost of £1200.

1913 — On quarterly exercise of the lifeboat, Mr William Thomas, a member of the local committee, had his left foot torn off through getting it caught in the quarter stopper. Committee of Management granted £500 to cover medical and other expenses.

1951 — Silver medals awarded to Second Coxswain William Dop, for his intrepid seamanship in the rescue of three people from the yacht *Waterbell* that was forced to anchor close to Porth Oer in a mass of breaking water on the night of the 8/9 August. The lifeboat arrived on scene half an hour after midnight in pitch dark and an increasing wind. The coxswain took her between the yacht and the rocks, which enabled the three men to jump aboard. He then brought the lifeboat out stern first and returned to station at 5.30am.

1964 — A Centenary Vellum awarded.

1975 — Bronze Medal awarded to Coxswain Griffith J. Jones, for the rescue of a man on the night of the 20 September seen clinging, in the dark, to a rock a quarter of a mile north of the lifeboat house. Using the lifeboat station's boarding boat, in strong gale force south-westerly winds and rough sea with a heavy swell, together with his son, he negotiated the narrow channels, reached the exhausted man and pulled him to safety aboard the boat. His 14-year-old son Eric, who also manned the boarding boat, was awarded an inscribed wristwatch.

1977 — Bronze Medal for gallantry awarded to crew member Glyn Roberts and the Thanks of the Institution inscribed on Vellum accorded to Second Coxswain Scott, for the rescue of a boy trapped 80 feet up the cliff face at Porth-y-Nant, on the night of 31 August / 1 September. Glyn Roberts and Second Coxswain John Scott launched the lifeboat at 11.15pm and went ashore in a boarding boat, between the dangerous rocks, in an eight foot swell. Glyn Roberts climbed up the cliff face to bring the boy to safety. A second boy was also reached from the beach.

1981 — Bronze Medal for gallantry awarded to Second Coxswain Michael Massarelli, in recognition of his courage, determination and seamanship when the lifeboat under his command rescued two men, who had been thrown into the water when their inflatable dinghy capsized and were clinging to the side, in Porthdinllaen Bay in north-easterly gale and a very rough sea on the afternoon of 25 April.

Porthdinllaen lifeboat Barbara Fleming *on the slipway c.1920.*
[Yvonne Edwards]

Medal Record:
One Silver and three Bronze Medals have been awarded, the last being voted in 1981.

Porthdinllaen Station Lifeboats
The first lifeboat to be received at Porthdinllaen on the Lleyn peninsula was launched in 1864, having been named the *Cotton Sheppard*. Crewed by twelve oarsmen, and with Hugh Hughes as coxswain until 1875, she had been adapted for her new role at a cost of £198. During her period at station, she was launched 26 times and rescued 43 persons. Her replacement, the new and larger *George Moore* lifeboat was launched 39 times and rescued 70 persons. She was followed by a second *George Moore*, a self-righting boat, which was in service between 1888 and 1902 and had cost £410. She was launched 11 times and rescued 22 persons. The *Barbara Fleming* lifeboat, which was on station from 1902 to 1926 and had cost £1277, was a 40 foot self-righting type and, during her period of service, was launched 32 times and saved 52 people. Amongst local vessels, which called for her assistance, were the schooner *Catherine and Margaret*, the ketch *Telephone*, the smack *Prosperity*, *County of Anglesey*, ketch *James*, schooner *Jane and Ann* and the fishing boat *Carry-Me-Safe*. The *Barbara Fleming* was followed by the *M O Y E* in service between 1926 and 1949. She cost £7614 and was launched 56 times and rescued 16 persons. The *Charles Henry Ashley*, in service between 1949 and 1979, cost £19,040 and was launched 151 times and rescued 89 persons. She was followed by the *Kathleen Mary* which cost £34,500 and was in service between 1979 and 1987. She was launched 53 times and rescued 28 persons. The present lifeboat, the *Hetty Rampton* was put into service in 1987. She is a 'Tyne' class self-righting boat and is driven by twin General Motor 6V-92 TI diesel engines which produce 425hp and a top speed of 18 knots. She was built by Fairey Allday Marine at Cowes at a cost of £508,696. In addition, the temporary lifeboats which have been on station from time to time, were launched 29 times and rescued 7 persons.

Name	Cost	Launches	Lives Rescued
Cotton Sheppard — 1864–77		26	43
George Moore — 1877–88		39	70
A second *George Moore* — 1888–1902	£ 410	11	22
Barbara Fleming — 1902–26	£ 1277	32	52
M.O.Y.E — 1926–49	£ 7614	59	16
Charles Henry Ashley — 1949–79	£19,040	168	95
Kathleen Mary — 1979–87	£34,500	62	29
Henry Rampton — 1987 to date	£508,696	-	-
Temporary lifeboats		29	7

Beaumaris and Penmon Lifeboat Station

Station History
The station was established in 1891 and closed in 1895 when Penmon was provided with a more powerful lifeboat. The station was re-opened in 1914.

Lifeboat Greater London II *photographed at Beaumaris. Back row L–R: RNLI official, M. Witkowski, D. W. Gallichan, M. Stone, L. Kopito, K. Charlton. Front row: B. Roberts, E. Jones, P. Kopito, G. Parry.*
[D. W. Gallichan]

1830 — Silver Medal awarded to David Griffiths, for the rescue, by rope, of 40 to 50 men, women and children from the emigrant ship *Newry*, that was wrecked off the Lleyn peninsula on 16 April 1830. The master ordered the mainmast cut down, to form a bridge between the ship and shore, thus saving 375 people, 40 to 50 of them by Mr Griffiths, with the help of three labourers who received a monetary award.

1831 — Silver Medals and Silver Boats awarded to William Lewis Walker and Ralph Williamson, for the rescue, by boat, of 22 people from the Steam Packet *Rothsay Castle* which was wrecked in horrendous weather on the night of 18 August. Over 120 people were lost.

1854 — The smack *Two Brothers* of Aberystwyth was, during a north easterly gale, stranded in Red Wharf Bay on the Anglesey coast. The crew of three men, after much difficulty and risk, were rescued by a shore boat manned by John Price and eight others. It was nearly four hours before the boat could reach the wreck, although the distance from the shore was not more than one mile. John Price was awarded a Silver Medal.

1911 — Lifeboat and slipway constructed at a cost of over £4,500.

1913 — King George V inspected the new lifeboat whilst it was at Cowes and took a trip on her.

1959 — A Letter of Appreciation, signed by the Chairman of the Institution, was sent to the coxswain and crew for standing by the Greek tanker *Essar I* throughout the night of 27/28 October in extremely severe weather conditions.

1967 — All weather lifeboat withdrawn from service. Inshore lifeboat station established in May with the placing on service of a D-Class lifeboat. The cost of the lifeboat was met by the BBC 'Blue Peter Appeal'.

1976 — D-Class lifeboat withdrawn and replaced with an Atlantic 21 lifeboat. The cost of the lifeboat was again met by the BBC 'Blue Peter Appeal'.

The Thanks of the Institution, inscribed on vellum, accorded to Helmsman John Charles Askew, in recognition of his services on 23 October, when the crew of two was rescued from the yacht *Tantivy*.

1978 — The Thanks of the Institution, inscribed on vellum, accorded to Helmsman David Jones, in recognition of his service on the Atlantic 21 lifeboat on 23 July 1977, when the yacht *Rosskop* was saved.

1982 — Bronze Medal was awarded to Coxswain David Gallichan, in recognition of the courage, judgement and seamanship displayed by him, when the lifeboat *Greater London II* (Civil Service No. 30) rescued the crew of the fishing vessel *Wygyr*, that was in difficulties at the northern end of the Menai Strait, in a strong south-south-easterly gale rising to storm force and a blizzard on 13 December 1981. The launch was found and taken in tow but, after the line parted, the two men were taken on board the lifeboat. A second attempt to tow the craft failed and she blew ashore and broke up. The two men were landed safely at Menai Bridge.

1983 – Atlantic 21 lifeboat-house extended to provide improved crew facilities.

1991 — Further extension to Atlantic 21 lifeboat house was constructed, to allow the housing of the lifeboat and launching tractor coupled in-line and, also, an integral souvenir sales outlet. The all weather lifeboat was withdrawn on 7 July and the station re-graded to all-year-round ILB station.

1998 — A Framed Letter of Appreciation, signed by the Chairman of the Institution, was awarded to crew member Martin Broughton, for the service to the yacht *Moon Storm*, which had gone aground in south-south-westerly winds which were Force 10/11 with recorded gusts of Force 12 with moderate seas, a six foot swell and poor visibility, in the early hours of the morning of the 24 October.

2000 — New boathouse completed May 2000. The new station B class lifeboat B768 was placed on service on 4 September 2000. This lifeboat was provided by the viewers of the BBC children's programme 'Blue Peter' and was funded from the proceeds of 'The Pieces of Eight Appeal', November 1993.

Medals:

Six Silver Medals and One Bronze Medal have been awarded, the last being voted in 1982.

Beaumaris Station Lifeboats

The first lifeboat to be stationed at Penmon in January 1830 was a 26^1/$_2$-foot rowing boat, capable of taking six oars and costing £43 11s. 0d. In August of the same year she was involved with the paddle-steamer *Rothesay Castle* when she ran aground on the Dutchman Bank. Of the 140 plus people on board, only twenty three survived, rescued by the lifeboat and other craft that assisted. Following on this disaster, the Trwyn Du lighthouse at Penmon was erected in 1838.

When the *Frederick Kitchin* arrived at Beaumaris in 1914, she was accommodated in a new station built on the outskirts of the town at a cost of £3,727 and which replaced the station at Penmon. She was a 'Watson' type of boat, with a 60bhp Tylor 'D' petrol engine, giving her a top speed of 7^1/$_2$ knots. The *Frederick Kitchin* was in fact the first motor lifeboat to be used at Beaumaris and was in service until 1945. Her replacement was *Field Marshall and Mrs Smuts* a 46ft x 12ft 9in 'Watson' class lifeboat with two 40bhp 'Ferry' VE4 diesel engines. She was built by Morgan Giles of Teignmouth at a cost of £13,865. It was on this boat that Coxswain Hugh Jones and his crew were called out when the tanker *Essar I* developed engine problems and began drifting near Point Lynas. Both the Beaumaris and Moelfre lifeboats were involved in standing by the vessel until she was taken on tow by a tug. The coxswain and his crew received a letter of appreciation from the chairman of the RNLI and, also, from the Beaumaris Town Council. On the 30 August 1966, Harold Jones became coxswain and continued in post until 1972, when William Pritchard took over from him. Five years later the *Field Marshall and Mrs Smuts* was withdrawn from service and replaced by the *Greater London II (Civil Service No. 30)* 46ft 9in 'Watson' Class lifeboat. Although she had been in service since being built in 1955, she had had new Watermota 'Sea-Lion' 70hp diesel engines fitted in 1969, which gave her a top speed of 8 knots. She was also fitted with radar.

When a call for assistance was received from the fishing launch *Wygyr* in December 1981, a force nine gale made the launching of the *Greater London II* extremely hazardous. With Coxswain David Gallichan, who had been appointed in June 1980, at the helm, the vessel was eventually found off Puffin Island. Not only had Coxswain

Gallichan to contend with a gale, which had now increased to storm force ten and gusting even higher, visibility was diminishing rapidly, due to the snow and ice piling against the windscreen and the wipers having stopped working. After an attempt at towing the *Wygyr* failed, due to the tow-line parting, Coxswain Gallichan skilfully brought the lifeboat alongside, sufficiently close to allow the two fishermen on board to leap on to the lifeboat. The two rescued men were landed at Menai Bridge. For outstanding seamanship, great courage and leadership, Coxswain Gallichan was awarded a Bronze Medal by the RNLI and Medal Service Certificates were presented to members of his crew.

When inflatable rescue boats were introduced by the RNLI in 1963, they were found to be ideal for rapid response when yachts and similar smaller craft were in trouble. As the result of an appeal, made on the BBC programme 'Blue Peter', sufficient monies were raised for a *Blue Peter II* IRB 127 to be made available at Beaumaris in 1967. These 15^1/$_2$-foot inflatable boats built of neoprene-proofed nylon were driven by a 40hp outboard-engine which could attain a speed of 20 knots. She was replaced, in 1976, by the B-515 Atlantic 21 class semi-rigid inflatable, which was driven by two 50hp outboard engines which gave her a speed of 30 knots when required. She had the benefit of a TW2 launching tractor and a new boathouse built near the pier. As the result of a rescue performed with this craft in October 1976, Helmsman John Askew was awarded the RNLI's Thanks on Vellum and Gareth Parry and Huw Williams Service Certificates on Vellum. When the full lifeboat service was withdrawn at Beaumaris in 1991, and the boathouse demolished a few months later, the rescue service continued with the Atlantic 21 Class *Blue Peter II*, B-563, which had been delivered in 1985 and continued in use until September 2000. The present Atlantic 75 Class B768 has twin outboard engines each developing 70hp.

Names	*Cost*	*Launches*	*Lives Rescued*
Tom and Jennie — 1891–95	£ 667	6	2
Previous station closed in 1895			
Frederick Kitchen — 1914—45	£ 3,727	38	46
Field Marshall and Mrs Smuts — 1945–76	£13,865	136	119
Greater London II — 1977–89	£32,188	38	21
The Robert — 1989–91	£34,826	2	1
Temporary lifeboats		21	8

The following anonymous poem, recited from memory by ninety-two year-old, double Gold Medal recipient Coxwain Richard Evans, OBE of Moelfre, exemplifies the attitudes of lifeboat crews in general.

Is there a path beneath the sea,
That leads to heaven above,
Does God wait there with outstretched hands,
To guide them with his love,
These stalwart men who face the deep,
And ride the raging sea,
Groping the dark of night,
To pull somebody free,
From the clutches of the biting cold,
Beneath the cruel waves,

Well aware that far below,
Are many watery graves,
Yet still they battle through the storm,
Whipped by the gale's full blast,
Tossed about in their tiny boats,
Until all hope is passed,
But some return to tell the tale,
Of those who died in vain,
To rescue those in peril,
To comfort those in pain,
Is there a path beneath the sea,
I wonder and I sigh when looking up at far off clouds,
So much like waves on high,
I feel that those who follow the path,
Sail on in God's great sea,
Chosen from the bravest ones,
To make God's heaven free,
From all the storms they faced on earth,
Each stark and bitter night,
Sailing into harbour now,
Guided by God's great light.

9. Wartime Activites

During the Second World War, travel within the Menai Strait was much more severely restricted, as indeed was the case along the entire British coastline. No vessel was allowed to enter or leave the ports of Caernarfon or Port Dinorwic during the hours of darkness. In the early part of the war, ships' officers were advised that they should have on board sufficient fuel and food, to enable them to proceed to the USA in the event of an invasion taking place. This applied to all vessels, irrespective of which port they happened to be in.

Coastal Protection

Even as early as 1938, Air Raid Precautions were being discussed at the Caernarfon Harbour Trust Office and, since this was listed as a Special Action Station, Air Ministry Air Raid Warning Exercises were carried out periodically in the period leading up to the war. In May 1939, further preparations were in hand:

> The Superintendent reported that inspection of the port and facilities had been made by an Inspector of the Air Defence Motor Patrol, Royal Arsenal, Woolwich, for the purpose of making arrangements to base one of the motor patrol boats to be stationed in Caernarvon Bay. It was expected that the boat would arrive in Caernarvon towards the end of the month … [C&DH, 5.5.39].

A letter from the Ministry of Transport, dated 2 March 1939, reminded harbour authorities of the danger of disclosing information concerning 'the working of British Dock and Harbour system … if it would assist a hostile power in time of war'. If information requested was generally available, i.e., published information, then it could be given but, in all other cases, requests were to be sent to the Ministry of Transport, to be dealt with through the Foreign Office [GAS XD15/30/94].

At the outbreak of the war, harbour authorities were obliged to carry out certain instructions issued by the Admiralty, including the extinguishing of all navigation lights and, in Caernarfon's case, the cessation of night traffic in and out of the port. A list of boat permits, with owners' names, and the names of boats permitted to operate on the Menai Strait, was displayed at the Harbour Office at Caernarfon.

The Harbour Trust was informed, on 6 November 1939, by the Commandant of the anti-aircraft artillery range at Tŷ Croes, Anglesey, that the camp was due to open on 11 November and requested that the Llanddwyn lighthouse keepers be allowed to hoist and/or lower a red flag at Llanddwyn, on receipt of instructions from the camp and also report the presence of shipping in the danger area [GAS, XD/15/3/6]. Instructions were also received from the Naval Officer in Charge at Holyhead, in December 1940, stating that the Llanddwyn lighthouse and associated walls had to be camouflaged in compliance with Admiralty orders [GAS, XD 15/21/4].

Drifting mines were a constant hazard during the war and one was observed by the coastguard on duty at Llanddwyn at 10.00am on 17 October 1941. The mine was driven on to nearby rocks, close to the lighthouse and the resulting explosion at 4.30pm damaged the door and roof of the lighthouse and smashed four windows.

Several more drifting mines were observed on 6 January 1942, some driven ashore at Llanddwyn and Abermenai beach and one drifting into the Strait, but they were all rendered ineffective by the mine disposal officer of the Admiralty.

In order that the Abermenai entrance to the Menai Strait, which was considered the most vulnerable, could be guarded, a flotilla of six motor patrol boats arrived on 6 July 1940, with the task of guarding the south entrance into Caernarfon harbour and patrolling the coast during the hours of darkness, as far south as Bardsey Island. These boats were based at Belan Point and moorings were laid there to accommodate them off the pier.

The Admiralty appointed Vice Admiral Hubert Lynes, RN (Retired) to be their Resident Naval Officer at the port of Caernarfon. Given the temporary rank of Commander, he was based at Bryn Gwyn, St. David's Road. An order which he issued on 2 July 1941 stated:

> … the south-western entrance to Menai Strait is closed to all Merchant Vessels, deep sea trawlers etc. For all ports in the Menai Strait, all such vessels must enter and leave the Strait by the north-eastern entrance only and obey the orders of the Examination Service Vessel there. The south western entrance is open only as follows — The Men of War who for every entry and exit will follow the procedure ordered for minor ports with Port War Signal stations (at Fort Belan). Llanddwyn light is temporarily extinguished and the tower and building are grey camouflaged. All the harbour lights at Caernarfon and Port Dinorwic are temporarily extinguished. The passage through the Strait is available for vessels up to about 260 feet long. But, even for small craft local knowledge is essential and only very small ones should attempt the passage except towards High Water Slacks … Passage beneath the Suspension Bridge or the Railway Tubular Bridge (by day or night) is prohibited, until permission has been received from the Menai Patrol, who will warn the military guard on the bridges. Failure to obtain permission to proceed will cause the offending vessel to be fired on … [GAS XD15/30/95].

In a secret document headed 'Menai Bridges Broken Down', dated July 1941, plans were made as to the type and number of boats required, to be available for transporting people across the Strait if, for any reason, either or both of the bridges became inoperative. In addition to the military guard on duty on the bridges, further protection against sabotage was provided by posting one policeman on duty on the centre spans of the Menai Suspension Bridge between 7.30am and 4pm and two from 4pm to 7.30am [GAS, XJ1234/11].

Detailed instructions, concerning guarding the approaches to the Menai Strait, were later issued by the Resident Naval Officer, Caernarfon, which stated that there would be two flotillas, each of six motor launches, operating from Caernarfon and Menai Bridge. The launches were of small cruiser-yacht type painted white and armed with a .303 machine-gun. It stated that '… these two Flotillas are to reinforce, inshore, the seaward watch and guard against INVASION which is being kept off this part of our coast …'. The Caernarfon Flotilla patrolled the area from Llanddwyn buoy towards Bardsey Island, while the Menai Bridge Flotilla patrolled between Great Orme and Lynas Point. In both cases, their role was to examine all craft approaching their respective entrances and '… ensure that they have no enemy troops, tanks, guns, or other war materials, or spies aboard them …'. The night patrol was expected to give 'early information of the approach of enemy invaders' and this they were expected to do with 'Firework Signals'. Three or more light rockets, which would have a bright light lasting seven seconds in the air, would indicate an 'enemy ship or other surface craft had been sighted'. If a large number of enemy aircraft were detected flying towards the shore, then one flash and sound rocket was to be fired. These rather vague instructions gave no indication as to how an 'enemy ship' or 'enemy aircraft' was to be identified, especially in the dark.

The launches had no means of communication, except at close range with voice or megaphone and semaphore hand-flags; they did not even have the benefit of a radio. It was expected that, whenever the rocket signal from the Caernarfon Flotilla was detected by the sentry post at Coed Helen army camp, Local Defence Volunteer Force (LDVF) (later to be re-named the Home Guard) or the Police, then they were to report the matter immediately to their respective headquarters. The Coastguard Stations and Coast Watch Posts were expected to report any sightings to the Naval Centre and, also, the Royal Naval Officer at Caernarfon. Any signals seen emanating from the Menai Bridge Flotilla, by the LDVF on the summit of Penmaenmawr mountain, or the Observer Corps on Great Orme, had to be reported to their respective headquarters. The Menai Bridge end of the Strait was covered by the LDVF at Red Wharf Bay, Police, Coastguard Stations and the Navy's Coast Watch Posts.

Having been advised in September 1939 that 1,000 sq yds. of the timber yard at the Victoria Dock in Caernarfon had to be reserved for the 'Mines Department', it came as no surprise when the Harbour Master was eventually told that the Admiralty had decided to lay a mine-field at the entrance of the Strait off Belan Point and that the mines would be of the ground type, weighing 2 tons each which could be fired from the shore. It was intended that the mine-field would be laid on 5 November 1940 at the Belan Narrows by HMS *Vernon* but, the work was postponed until 3 March 1941, when HMS *Bennevis* called to ratify the area to be mined and the work was carried out on 20 March 1941 by HMS *M4*.

Similar mines, placed alongside the sea wall from a position off the Old Battery to the Oil Wharf and buried below the surface of the sea bed, could have been fired from the shore. Additional precautions were taken with the military erecting two pill boxes — one alongside the old battery and the other abreast of the timber yard at Victoria Dock. Once the mine-field had been laid the flotilla of patrol boats was withdrawn [GAS XD 15/21/4]. Belan Fort was also the base for the RAF Air-Sea Rescue boats and the location of naval guns as additional precaution against unauthorised entry into the Menai Strait.

Although Caernarfon was considered to be comparatively safe from bombing, on 4 May 1943 the Harbour Trust took delivery of a light fire-fighting trailer pump, for use within the port area, and further precautions had to be taken, such as the camouflage of the oil tanks adjoining the Victoria Dock, so as to be 'invisible' from the air.

With the possibility of oil supplies being disrupted by enemy action, additional tanks were installed underground at the old brickworks at Parkia, Griffith's Crossing and, on 5 August 1941, petrol began to be pumped through a 4" pipe laid by the War Department from Caernarfon to the new Shell depôt, where a petrol can filling facility had been installed. Thereafter, whenever a delivery of petrol was made to Caernarfon by ship, it was immediately pumped through to Griffith's Crossing. These new oil installations enabled high octane petrol, suitable for planes, to be stored prior to distribution to nearby airfields. A periodic inspection of the sea outlets took place at Griffith's Crossing by the Harbour Trust and the Fisheries Patrol Officer for signs of oil pollution into the Strait.

The facilities provided at Port Dinorwic dry-dock together with the workforce expertise, were used extensively during the war, with many vessels, especially those damaged by enemy action, being repaired. Often, because of the extent of the damage inflicted, a ship had to be assisted into the port, as was the case with the mine-sweeper HMS *En Avour*, which was towed by the Caernarfon Harbour Trust vessel, *Seiont II*, from Bangor on 1 April 1941 [GAS, XD 15/21/4].

At nearby Dinas, Port Dinorwic, Dowsett-Mackay Engineering Construction Co. Ltd. (or Dow-Mac as it was generally known) had taken over the old shipbuilding yard and erected a large shed over it. There they assembled steel sections to form 40 foot, flat-bottomed tugs, powered by a twin-screw petrol engine and a small open wheelhouse aft, for towing barges of similar size for use as supply boats in the Persian Gulf waterways. When completed, sea trials were held against a measured mile between Rowen Bay, Felinheli and Llanfairisgaer along the Menai Strait. The barges were then stacked along the foreshore at Felinheli (Port Dinorwic), prior to being transported by low-loader to Liverpool for onward shipment. Steel sections for the barges were stored at Ala Las, and St. Helens Road, Caernarfon.

With the threat of invasion past and the end of the war in Europe in sight, permission was given early in 1945 for the Llanddwyn Island light, as with other navigation lights around the coast, to be 're-exhibited at normal characteristics and full brilliancy'.

Saunders Roe, Beaumaris

As the result of enemy action at Cowes, Isle of Wight, the marine aviation company Saunders Roe decided, in September 1940, to move its design department to the comparative safety of a property known as 'Fryers', which the company had purchased a mile from Beaumaris on the east side of Anglesey. The office staff were housed in the main house, whilst various sheds and hangars, some of which had been brought from Cowes, were erected in the surrounding 50 acres of land. A concrete apron, extending into the nearby Menai Strait, allowed amphibious aircraft to be hauled ashore. The company was able to exploit its flying-boat expertise when it was awarded a contract, in 1940, by the Ministry of Aircraft Production, the organisation responsible for placing orders on behalf of the British Government.

In 1940, aircraft manufacturers in America and Canada had been asked to carry out certain technical changes to Catalina, Kingfisher, Coronado, Seamew and Mariner aircraft so as to conform with RAF requirements but, because of delays in delivery, this arrangement was changed in favour of carrying out alterations in this country. When changes were carried out to aircraft in America, they were described as 'modifications', whereas those carried out in this country were 'alterations'. Production planning, with regard to the number or type of aircraft due to arrive, was extremely difficult, if not impossible. It was even found, on some occasions, that alterations

Consolidated Catalina on the slipway at Saunders Rowe, Fryars, Beaumaris, during the Second World War. [W. Williams]

programmed to be carried out on planes arriving from America had already been carried out during manufacture.

The first Catalina, a monoplane flying boat with retractable wing tip floats, was flown from America at the end of February 1941, to be handled by Scottish Aviation Ltd. at Greenock on the Clyde. For a number of reasons, it was decided that future work would be diverted to Beaumaris, but, until the slipway was completed in April 1941 and aircraft could be hauled out of the water, work on the Catalinas was carried out whilst moored to one of the many special buoys, which extended over several miles along the Strait (creating another hazard which shipping had to be wary of).

As soon as space became available ashore, the aeroplane would be brought from its mooring into the factory, where a number of tasks were performed, including the removal of the extra fuel tanks installed inside the hull for its flight from Goose Bay to Beaumaris.

Appendix I — Felinheli Mariners

The following mariners who were associated with the village have not been compiled as a definitive list. Every effort has been taken to ensure accuracy, but detail shown has, of necessity, been extracted from a variety of sources. The author would be pleased to be advised of any inadvertent errors. The final figure appearing in many of the entries indicates the age of the person when he died.

Capt. Joseph Acton, 14 July 1862, 53

Capt. Thomas Maurice Acton, 24 January 1888, 54

Engineer Charles James Bowles, Merchant Navy, Second World War

PO Charles Henry Butler, First World War

William Caddock, 73 Bangor Street

Chief Officer John Cecil Chubb

Sidney Mons Chubb, 10 October 1942, 27, Merchant Navy, Second World War

Daniel Davies, 3 Moelydon Terrace

Capt. John Davies, Frondirion, 26 October 1893, 61

John Davies, Merchant Navy, Second World War

Capt. J. W. Davies, 1870–1939

Capt. Lewis Davies, *Harriette Preston*, January 1883, 44

Robert Davies, Harbour Master, 17 March 1915, 62

Chief Officer Peter Dop, *Linda Blanche*, Second World War

Captain Robert Dop, MV *St Tudno*

Capt. Richard Edwards, Wern, Llanfairisgaer 26 July 1900, 61

Robert Edwards, 16 August 1856, 48

Thomas Edwards, 1 March 1867, 26

William Edwards, Trinity Pilot, 21 June 1904, 65

Capt. John Elias, 1 Port Terrace, 3 October 1889, 63

Capt. Owen Elias, Bodawain, 25 January 1924, 74

William Morris Elias, 1 Port Terrace

Capt. Henry Ellis, 26 April 1880, 72

John Ellis, Menai Street, 27 October 1892, schooner *Annie*

Capt. John Ellis, 19 April 1899, 48

PO John Ellis, Bryn Melyn, Royal Naval Volunteer Reserve, First World War

Capt. John Ellis, 41 Bangor Street, 1919

Chief Officer William Ellis, Merchant Navy, Second World War, 1901–42

Capt. Henry Evans, Boston Street, schooner *Annie*, 27 October 1892

Robert Evans, 28 Beach Row, schooner *Bodecia*, 5 March 1890, 22

Thomas Evans, 31 May 1866, 57

Capt. William Evans, 11 Port Terrace, 4 March 1925, 93

Capt. William Evans, SS *Elidir*, 19 August 1951, 85

Chief Officer, William Favretto, Merchant Navy, Second World War

Capt. Henry Francis, 9 Port Terrace, 5 March 1890

Capt. Alex Grant, Pen y Wern, 3 February 1924, 80

John Griffiths

Llewellyn Griffith, Tanymaes, Royal Navy, First World War

Capt. Owen Griffiths, 21 May 1896, 77

William Hatton, 6 Menai Street

Richard Hayward, 6 September 1885, 19

Walter Horlock, 60 Bangor Street

Edward Hughes

Chief Officer Herbert Ellis Hughes, Merchant Navy, Second World War

Capt. Hugh Hughes, 6 Sea View Terrace, 1901

John Hughes, 6 Helen Terrace, Royal Navy, First World War

Richard Hughes, Merchant Navy, Second World War

Capt. William Hughes, Bangor Street, SS *Penrhyn*, 1953

William Humphreys, Augusta Place, 24 August 1935, 78;

Capt. David Jones, Menai Hill, 5 May 1874, 75

PO David Jones, Royal Naval Reserve, First World War

Ellis Jones, sailor, Snowdon Street, 21 June 1884, 65

Capt. Evan Jones, Gorphwysfa, 1882, 65

Francis Jones, Aber Cottage, 24 July 1867, 25

Griffith Jones, 9 Menai Street, 5 January 1932, 67

Capt. Griffith Jones, 2 Bangor Street, 1884, 54

Capt. Griffith Jones, Bodafon, November 1945

Henry Jones, Alice Davies, 21 November 1878, 17

Henry Jones, Beach Road, *Restless*, 23 August 1895

Capt. Henry Jones, Awelfryn, 10 October 1933, 74

Capt. Hugh Jones, 13 Menai Street, 16 September 1913, 83

John Jones, 1 Augusta Place

John Jones, Glanhwfa, 19 February 1907, 37

Chief Officer John Jones, 1885

Capt. John Jones, Mona House, Bessie Rowe, 3 August 1878, 57

Capt. John Jones, The Moorings, 11 October 1911, 43

Capt. John Jones, Menai Street, SS *Enid*, 2 November 1926, 79

Capt. J. Jones, Minnie Coles

Capt. J. Jones, Bush Road

J. D. Jones, Port Cottage, SS *Englishman*

Capt. John Hughes Jones, 12 Menai Street, 15 October 1924, 72

John Morris Jones, Merchant Navy, Second World War

Capt. John T. Jones, Menai Street, 14 April 1894, 28

John Theophilus Jones, 19 Beach Road

Capt. Owen Jones, Alun Terrace, 16 November 1885, 55

Capt. Owen John Jones, Y Dderwen, 16 July 1974

Capt. R. Jones, schooner *Fairy*

Capt. Richard Jones, 18 May 1865, 52

Capt. Richard Jones, Bryn Goleu, 19 January 1909, 72;

Robert Jones, 16 January 1886, 73

Capt. R. E. Jones, Cartref, 6 March 1929

Capt. R. O. Jones, The Cliff

R. W. Jones, Augusta Place, SS *George*, 29 January 1907, 30

Capt. Theophilus Jones, Snowdon Street, schooner *Venerable*, 1836–88

Capt. Thomas S. Jones, Sea View Terrace, 16 October 1885, 60

William Jones, 9 March 1840, 52

Capt. W. Jones, Bronfa, Bangor Street

Capt. William Jones, Frondeg Terrace, 1869, 52

Capt. William Jones, schooner *Commodore*, 11 March 1890, 90

Capt. William Jones, Port Dinorwic, schooner *Emily Louisa*, 7 April 1890, 44

Capt. William Jones, 3 December 1910, 48

Capt. William Jones, Velinheli Terrace, SS *Dinorwic*, 14 February 1915, 43

William Jones, Snowdon Street, 10 March 1915, 40

Capt. William Jones, Bodlondeb, 1963

William Richard Jones, Mercantile Marine, First World War

Capt. W. R. Jones, Bodwyn, 1933

Capt. David Lewis, 11 Port Terrace, 21 March 1884, 65

Capt. Lewis Lewis, Glanhwfa, 14 January 1931, 73

Capt. Thomas Lillie, 16 June 1949, 83

Andrew Maguire, 21 Snowdon Street, SS *Elidir*, 19 October 1913, 50

Richard Maguire, 21 Snowdon Street, 15 July 1942, 34

William Richard Maguire, Merchant Navy, Second World War

Donald Mackay, 1 June 1865, 55

Griffith Morgan, Menai Street, schooner *Annie*, 27 October 1892, 21

John Morris, 1 July 1940, 49, *Arandora Star*

David Owen, 29 January 1868, 55

Emlyn Owen, AB, Merchant Navy, Second World War

Goronwy Owen, AB, Merchant Navy, Second World War

Hugh T. Owen, Mona Terrace

Lewis Owen

Capt. Richard Owen, Augusta Place

Capt. Owen Owens, Halfway, 28 October 1892, 60

Walter Palmer, SS *Elidir*, 20 April 1993, 96

Capt. Owen Parry, 18 May 1879, 62

Capt. Rice Parry, Angorfa, 16 August 1911

Capt. Richard Parry, Mona Terrace, 31 July 1915, 89

Capt. Robert Parry, SS *Alliance*, 20 Bangor Street, 4 June 1898, 58

Robert William Parry, Royal Navy, HMS *Defence*, 31 May 1916, 26

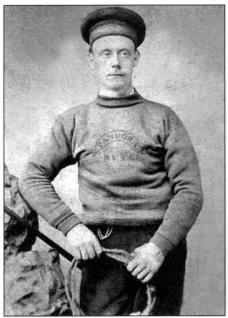

The young Thomas Wilson Roberts as a crew member of the SY Pandora. *[Elsbeth Pritchard]*

Captain John Williams [Port Dinorwic Historical Society]

Lewis Owen. He initially served with the Blue Funnel Line before joining DQ ships. A fine amateur artist. [John Bryan Owen]

Capt. Thomas Henry Parry, 1912, 58

Thomas John Parry

Capt. William Parry, Port Terrace, schooner *Menai*, 15 October 1874, 52

William Parry, Bryn Ffynnon Road, 2 May 1915, 57

Capt. William Parry, Brynffynnon, schooner *Catherine*, 31 October 1905, 78

David Pierce, Boston Terrace, RMS *Loanda*, 30 June 1895, 43

Henry R. Pierce, Trinity Pilot, 33 Beach Road, 6 May 1918, 48

John Pierce 13 April 1874, 21

John Pierce, 33 Beach Road, 15 November 1907, 82

Richard Pierce, 27 September 1887, 27

Richard Pierce, Dinas

Capt. Robert Pierce, 22 Bangor Street

William Pierce, 20 Beach Road

John L. Pritchard, Annie, 27 October 1892, 19

Llywelyn Prichard, Royal Naval Reserve, First World War

Capt. David Pugh, Menai Street, 29 June 1893, 69

Capt. Edward Pugh, 14 January 1864, 34

Capt. Joseph Richardson, 1826–85

Capt. David Roberts, 15 Terfyn Terrace, 6 April 1941, 72

Capt. Edward Roberts, Treflys, 3 January 1944, 64

Evan Roberts, 4 Terfyn Terrace, 1883, 15

Capt. Evan Roberts, Snowdon Street, 21 November 1879, 33

Capt. Griffith Roberts, 4 Terfyn Terrace, 8 November 1903, 79

John Roberts, Pilot, 1892, 77

Capt. John Roberts, *Antelope*, 15 January 1913, 74

Capt. John Roberts, 9 Port Terrace, 11 December 1914, 57

Capt. John Roberts, 59 Bangor Street

J. O. Roberts, Efrog House

John Robert Roberts, Bryn Alun, Royal Navy, First World War

Capt. Owen Roberts, Menai Street, 6 April 1898, 78

Capt. Richard Ellis Roberts, 13 March 1883, 49

Robert Roberts, 9 May 1851, 42

Capt. Robert Roberts, 25 July 1851, 47

Capt. Robert Roberts, Mona View, 24 July 1900, 38

Capt. Robert Ellis Roberts, 13 March 1885, 49

Thomas Roberts, Menai Street schooner *Annie* 27 October 1892

Capt. Thomas Wilson Roberts, Bodawel, 1857–1937

Capt. William Roberts, schooner *Margaret & Martha*, 11 September 1871, 66

Capt. William Roberts, schooner *Edward Beck*, 16 May 1876, 42

Capt. William Roberts, 4 Terfyn Terrace, 1883, 30

Capt. William Roberts, *Ocean Maid*, 16 January 1894, 67

Ellis Thomas, Tyn y Cae, 19 June 1897, 65.

Capt Henry Thomas, Awelfryn, 10 October 1933, 74

Capt. John Thomas, Estate Yard Cottage, 24 February 1911, 40

Capt. Joseph Thomas, Menai Street, 1873, 45

Capt. Robert David Thomas, September 1914

Capt. Robert David Thomas, Menai Street, 2 April 1930, 44

Thomas Thomas, Pilot, 1879, 80

Capt. William Thomas, 1 Menai Street, *Galloway Lass*, 3 June 1875, 43

Capt. John Joseph Tildsley, Bryn Melyn, Merchant Navy, 1871–1959

Capt. Ben Williams, Hafan 1876-1952

Capt. D. G. Williams, Halfway, 5 April 1986, 80

Capt. Evan Williams, brig *Ellinor*, 19 April 1831, 26

Glynn George Williams, 1899–1981, Royal Navy

Capt. Griffith Williams, *Catherine Roberts*, 13 August 1888, 54

Petty Officer Gwilym Williams, Royal Navy

Capt. Hugh Williams, *Cambrian Queen*, 20 March 1894, 35

Capt. Hugh Williams, Caegwyndryn, 24 December 1913, 56

John Williams, Monfa, Mercantile Marine, *Connemara*, 3 November 1916, 22

Capt. John Williams, 15 Florence Terrace, 3 January 1890, 51

Capt. John Williams, Helen Terrace, *Cambria*, 12 March 1907, 56

Capt. John Williams, SS *Alistair*, 20 December 1907, 53

John Williams, 18 Menai Street, 5 March 1909, 54

Lewis Williams, 8 September 1917, 64

Owen Williams, 3 March 1888, 47

Owen Williams, 31 May 1888, 21

Capt. Owen Williams, 10 Bangor Street, 22 July 1894, 29

Capt. Owen Williams, 5 Sea View Terrace, steamship *Monarch*, 1873–1908

PO Owen Williams, Merchant Navy, Second World War

Capt. Owen Williams, *Ferndale*, 23 March 1928

Owen Glyn Williams, 30 Bangor Street

Owen Lewis Williams, 4 August 1891, 20

Capt. Robert Williams, Augusta Place, 16 February 1876, 38

Robert Williams, 5 Sea View Terrace, schooner *Annie*, 27 October 1892, 13

Capt. Robert Williams, 30 Bangor Street

Robert Arthur Williams, 30 Bangor Street

Thomas J. Williams, 8 Snowdon Street, 1941, 34

Capt. Thomas O. Williams, 14 Helen Terrace, Merchant Navy, 6 March 1942, 65

William Williams, 15 August 1861, 25

William Williams, 5 Sea View, Royal Navy, First World War

William Williams, 2 Beach Road, 23 December 1924, 74

Capt. William Williams, PS *Snowdon*, 1941

Capt. W Williams, Islwyn

Capt. William David Williams, 1905–52 SS *Velinheli*

William Grey Williams, 30 Bangor Street, Royal Navy

William Pugh Williams, 23 Bangor Street, 10 January 1929, 80

Examples of ships that Port Dinorwic men served on:

Alice 22190	– William Davies, AB, aged 30, previously *Bodicea*
Ann and Laura 24668	– William Jones, 30, mate, previously *William Bowden*
Becky Sharp 62847	– William Edwards, boy, 16, 1873
Canadian 113425	– Robert Jones, AB, 24, previously *Peleus* 1903
Ellen 29222	– Daniel Edwards, AB, 48, previously *Margaret* 1873
	– William Evans, master, 42
	– Henry Hughes, AB, 44, previously *William* 1877
Fairy 17563	– John Lewis, AB, 28, previously *Amiable* 1881
	– Griffith Roberts, 15, boy, previously *Planet* 1881
	– Owen Roberts, boy, 15, previously *Penmaen* 1881
Gleaner 20238	– Hugh Roberts, master, 23, 1876
Isabella 76889	– John Roberts, OS, b1875, previously *Vaynol* 1893
Kate 63917	– Thomas Williams — master, 45, previously *Winifred*
Lady Elizabeth 81576	– Wm. Hughes, AB, b.1841, previously *Thauma*
	– T. Williams, AB, b.1841, previously *North Cambria*
Llanelly 60772	– David Owens, AB, b.1860, previously *Ninadria* 1892
Louis Napoleon 33266	– John Jones, mate, 31 previously *Eleanor Thomas*
	– John Roberts, AB, 18 previously *Eleanor Thomas*
	– John Williams, OS, 17 previously *Eleanor Thomas*
Louise 76305	– John Lewis, AB, b.1854
Margaret and Mary 27434	– John Roberts, OS, 19, previously *Progress* 1874
Merle 48592	– Robert A. Roberts, master, b.1843
Port Antonio 111315	– William Hughes, 2nd engineer, 29
Pursuit 44244	– William Jones, master, 26

– Hugh Williams, OS/cook, 15, previously *Wepre Lass*

Queen Victoria — John Roberts, AB, b1871

Royal Charter 21322 — Edward Edwards, AB, 20, previously *Batavia* 1873

Seven Brothers 56213 — W. Humphreys, mate, 22, previously *Eleanor and Jane* 1876

Snaefell 44724 — Daniel Edwards, AB, 26, previously SS *Voltaic*

William 29226 — William Edwards, OS, 18, previously *Mary Rowlands*

– W. Edwards, OS, 21, previously *Elizabeth and Mary*

– Edward Edwards, mate, 21, previously *Ellen*

– Henry Jones, boy, 14 (first voyage)

– Thomas Jones, master, 50, previously *William*

– William Jones, OS, 17, previously *Climax* 1875

– Robert Richards, mate, 19, previously *Progress*

– Humphrey Williams, mate, 45, previously *William*

Xanthus 29327 — William Parry, 24, previously *Catharina*

– Hugh Roberts, 16, previously *Mary Rowlands*

Appendix II — Ships built at Port Dinorwic

Year	Name	Type	Tonnage	Fate
1849	*Palestine*	Schooner	113 tons	lost April 1855
1850	*Harriet Preston*	Schooner	58	lost 1865
1853	*Mary Coles*	Schooner	95	lost Point Lynas
1855	*John Preston*	Schooner	120	lost 1882
1857	*Jane Hughes*	Schooner	94	lost 1859
1858	*Jennett Evans*	Schooner	100	sold in Ireland
1858	*Menai*	Schooner	96	lost 1901
1859	*Margaret and Mary*	Schooner	100	lost Land's End
1859	*William Keith*	Schooner	99	lost 1906
1860	*Arvon*	Schooner	100	lost 1875
1861	*Ward Jackson*	Schooner	97	lost near Cardiff
1861	*Emily Louisa*	Schooner	71	sold in Ireland
1862	*Dinorwic*	Schooner	124	torpedoed 1917
1862	*Infanta*	Schooner	45	lost off Kent
1864	*Atlanta*	Brigantine	223	lost 1892
1865	*Vanguard*	Schooner	95	sold 1874
1866	*Latona*	Barque	286	sold 1881
1867	*Minnie Coles*	Schooner	115	torpedoed 1918
1868	*Camelot*	Barque	345	lost
1870	*Palestine*	Brigantine	223	lost 1892
1871	*Becky Sharp*	Smack	40	lost 1876
1871	*Maggie Woodburne*	Schooner	108	fate unknown
1873	*A. M. Rowlands*	Brigantine	176	sold in Amlwch
1877	*Ordovic*	Barque	860	lost Cape Horn
1878	*Velinheli*	Schooner	65	sold 1909
1880	*Miss Williams*	Schooner	79	lost 1906
1886	*Ruby*	Ketch	44	sold
1895	*E. E. Muspratt*	Ketch	80	sold in Liverpool
1897	*Empress Climax*	Ketch	80	beached locally

Appendix III — Port Dinorwic Docks

Extracts from 1902 Paper, 3296, by Frank Oswell, BA, Assoc. M. Inst. CE

Port Dinorwic was formerly called Felinheli, meaning 'sea-water mill', from a mill that existed there about a century ago which is said to have been worked by the tides presumably by impounding the flood-water and using it as the tide fell. The foundations of the mill were found in the course of the present work at the site indicated in old estate plans.

The inner part of the creek was then little more than a marsh with a stream trickling through it. Part of the foreshore near the mouth was reclaimed and converted into a quay and a tidal dock in 1797 by walls of roughly-squared limestone laid without mortar and backed in the roughest-hewn slate slabs, 5 inches to 10 inches in thickness and as much as 11 feet or 12 feet in length. Later on the dock was continued up the creek with walls of similar construction to a point near the entrance of the present dry dock. The old quays were for the most part made ...of such loose materials as slate rubbish, sea sand, copper dross (from the old mines at Amlwch) and rough stones. They were therefore nearly as porous as the walls and the water admitted to the back of the walls during flood-tide escaped so readily as the tide fell that the walls stood fairly well, although, from bad foundations and rough construction, they had in course of time bulged and settled and lost alignment in some places to a dangerous extent.

The older part of the harbour occupying the foreshore, has been left as it was, the new works being wholly beyond the crown boundary on property belonging to the owner of the Dinorwic slate quarries, Mr G. W. Duff Assheton-Smith, at whose private expense the works were carried out ... . The new works were rendered necessary by the inadequacy of the old dock to deal with the output of the quarry which has greatly increased in recent years. The chief requirement was extension of quay-space to provide stocking-ground in dull times and with this object, since only one side of the dock is available for loading, the width of water has been limited generally to such as is sufficient to allow two vessels to pass each other the rest of the available space being converted into quays ... . Much delay in loading and considerable detriment to boats were caused by grounding as the tide fell; it was therefore determined to retain the water in the new docks by means of a lock and ultimately it was decide to complete the scheme by the addition of a dry dock and repairing-shops large enough to deal with any boat in the trade ... . Since strangers using the port, and not only vessels belonging to the proprietor, will be admitted to the dry-dock, it is expected to pay well for itself, no such accommodation having hitherto been available nearer than the ship-canal. A profitable return on the cost of the rest of the works will be derived from the avoidance of dues and other heavy expenses connected with the old port, not to speak of the great advantages arising from its improvement and extension.

The contractor whose tender was accepted began work in April 1897 but it was found necessary after 7 months to terminate the contract, the Author carrying on the work without a contractor from that time until its completion in December 1900.

Temporary Works – A cofferdam to shut out the sea was built across the entrance to the creek which was only about 70 feet in width. It was bonded into the old quay-wall at the south end and was carried on benchings up the sloping rock at the north end ... . Two large sluices were provided near the bottom of the dam and a 13-inch Gwynne centrifugal pump was fixed about 15 feet below the top of the dam to drain the works. The boiler used in connection with this pump was that of the locomotive which fell down the mountain side in the Snowdon Railway accident in April 1896... (Both pump and boiler) are now established for permanent service at the dry-dock.

Foundations: ... In all parts of the excavations even deep down in the blue clay were found the remains of oak and other trees some of them oak logs being still quite sound although they must have lain there for many centuries. A hard clay-shale found at the north side of the dry dock was strongly impregnated with copper and was believed to overlie rich ore.

Masonry: All angles excepting hollow quoins are of limestone from Traeth Bychan, a quarry in Anglesey which produces stone of exceptionally good quality. The quoins are uniformly five courses in height ... excepting in the dry dock where they are six courses in height ... . The coping is from the same quarry and consists of blocks alternately 2 feet 6 inches and 3 feet on the bed, 12 inches thick and 3 feet to 9 feet in length ... Bollards of the hook pattern weighing 8 cwts. each were fixed at the edge of the coping about 50 feet apart on the south side and between that distance and 100 feet apart on the other side. Each end of the lock is furnished with a larger and heavier pair of the same type. They are anchored into the concrete with four long bolts raking in both directions provided with cast-iron plates and cottars at the end. At every berth wrought-iron ladders are fixed in chases left for them in the face of the wall and the lock is furnished with two such ladders.

The Lock: The length adopted of 180 feet between the sills is fully sufficient for the vessels using the Port which do not exceed 150 feet in length over all. Vessels which are too long for the lock can pass through on the top of any tide that is high enough to open the gates. The peculiar form of the north side of the entrance is due to the necessity of keeping the walls clear of the Crown boundary ... . The gates are of greenheart and the small width of the opening (32 feet) rendered the simple section...fully adequate. To check any tendency to drop at the mitre each gate is fitted with a pair of diagonal tie-rods of $1^3/_8$ inch round iron with stretching-screws for adjusting. There are foot-bridges of the usual pattern across each pair of gates. The gate-machines are winches fixed in chambers below the coping and worked by capstans above. The middle of a chain is wrapped round the barrel of the winch and the ends are led over the two sides of each gate and made fast to lewis-bolts, one in the floor on the outer side, the other in a recess at the back of the gate and the gate is opened or closed by winding the winch backwards and forwards. The gates and their equipment were made and erected by Messrs Cleghorn and Wilkinson of Northwich.

The Dry Dock: ... The walls are of concrete 11 feet in thickness at floor-level battering 1 foot on the face up to the first altar about 4 feet above. There are three ladders on each side recessed into the walls and a double flight of steps and a timber-slide at the end ... Two Gwynne centrifugal pumps, one 13-inch and one 8-inch capable of delivering together nearly 5,000 gallons per minute are fixed in a chamber under the coping at the south side of the entrance ... . The keel-blocks which were cast in the quarry shops, are of the Mersey Harbour Board pattern but rather smaller and lighter than those used in Liverpool. They raise the keel 3 feet above the floor and are spaced 4 feet 6 inches apart centre to centre excepting the last seven at the stern end which are spaced 4 feet 4 inches apart ... . The entrance is closed by a steel falling-gate hinged at the bottom, this form being chosen in order to save space ... . Repairing-shops of steel frame-work made specially heavy in order to carry shafting ... was supplied and erected by Messrs Bruce and Still of Liverpool ... (it can) accommodate four of the small quay locomotives ... . A road which formerly crossed the dock by a swing bridge is now carried by a lifting-bridge to economise space. This was built and erected by Messrs Pearson and Knowles of Warrington.

Appendix IV — Piracy and Smuggling

Piracy came in two forms: a ship described as a privateer, fitted out, as the name implies, privately, was licensed by the government to seize enemy ships and cargo on the high seas. Whereas a pirate whose ship, free to roam the high seas without any legal authority, would plunder any vessel, whether it be friend or foe, without any legal authority, government or otherwise.

Undoubtedly, the greater part of goods transported by sea was of a legitimate nature but, smuggling and even piracy was certainly not unknown in west Wales. The armed cruiser, the *Fox*, operating between Anglesey and the Bristol Channel, smuggled tea and casks of spirits in 1773. Similar operations were carried out by an Aberaeron boat the *Swallow* in 1757.

Revenue cutters, such as the *Hector* of about 100 tons and carrying some 45 men, were never very successful in preventing the smuggling of tobacco, brandy, tea, wine and gin being landed along the coast between Ynys Enlli (supposedly a holy island but used as a base for piracy in the sixteenth century) and the Dee partly because there were, at that time, literally hundreds of small craft plying up and down the north Wales coast carrying a variety of goods.

Salt, an essential commodity in the herring industry, was also smuggled between Ireland and Wales because of the difference in price, 4d. per lb in this country compared to 1d. per lb in Ireland. When slate was exported to Ireland, salt was often hidden on board under ballast of stone and sand on the return voyage to Wales. Even though the risks and penalties for smuggling were always high, the rewards were equally as great.

Select Bibliography

Bassett, T. M. & B. L. Davies, *Atlas of Caernarvonshire* (Gwynedd Rural Council), 1977.

Barker, D. S. 'Cruising the North Wales Coast', *Sea Breezes*, September, 1988.

Chatterton, E. Keble, *Q-ships and Their Story*, Sidgwick & Jackson, 1922.

Dodd, A. H., *A History of Caernarvonshire, 1284–1900*, Caernavonshire Historical Society, 1968.

Eames, Aled, *Ships and Seamen of Gwynedd*, Gwynedd ARchives Service, 1976.

Eardley-Wilmot, J. E., *A Famous Fox Hunter — Reminiscences of Thomas Assheton Smith*, 1859.

Fenton, R. S., *Mersey Rovers*, World Ship Society, Gravesend, 1997.

    Cambrian Coasters, World Ship Society, Kendal, 1989.

Hall, Edmund Hyde, *A Description of Carnarvonshire 1809–1811*, Gwenlyn Evans, 1952.

Harper, C. G., *The Holyhead Road*, II, Chapman & Hall, 1902.

Hemmingway, J., *Panorama of the Beauties, Curiousities and Antiquities of North Wales*, R. Groombridge, London, 1835.

Jones, Reg Chambers, *Arian – the story of money and banking in Wales*, Christopher Davies, 1978.

    Bless 'Em All — Aspects of the War in north-west Wales, 1939–45, Bridge Books, 1995.

    Bridges and Ferries, Christopher Davies, 1975.

    Curiouser and Curiouser — oddities in north-west Wales, Bridge Books, 1998.

    Felinheli — A Personal History of the Port of Dinorwic, Bridge Books, 1992.

Jones, Richard J., *The Loss of HMS Conway*, privately published, n.d.

Lewis, E. A., *Welsh Port Books, 1550–1603*, Hon. Society of Cymmrodorion, 1927.

Lloyd, Lewis, *The Port of Caernarfon 1793–1900*, Gwasg Pantycelyn, Caernarfon, 1989.

Masefield, John, *Extracts from The Conway*, Heineman Ltd, 1933.

Morton, H. V., *In Search of Wales*, Methuen & Co. Ltd., 1933.

Pritchard, Dylan, 'The Slate Trade in North Wales', unpublished thesis, University College of North Wales, Bangor, 1935.

Pritchard, R. T. 'The Post Road in Caernarvonshire — An Historical Survey', *Transactions*, Caernarvonshire Historical Society, XIII, 1952.

Roberts, Captain D. '40 Years Ago', *Sea Breezes*, VIII, 1949.

Rolt, L. T. C., *Thomas Telford*, Longmans, Green & Co., 1958.

Stammers, Michael K., *A Maritime Fortress*, University of Wales Press, 1949.

Thomas, David, *Hen Longau a Llongwyr Cymru*, University of Wales Press, 1952.

Thomas, David, 'Hen Longau Sir Gaernarfon', Caernarvonshire Historical Society, Gwenlyn Evans, Caernarfon, 1952.

Thornley, F. C., *Steamers of North Wales*, T. Stephenson & Sons Ltd., 1962.

Turner, Sir Llewelyn, *The Memories of Sir Llewelyn Turner*, Ibister, 1903.

Waine, Charles V., *Steam Coasters and Short Sea Traders*, Research Publications, 1976.

Williams, M. Elis, 'Samuel Roberts: Preacher and Shipbuilder, 1819–1875', *Cymru a'r Môr*, IX, Gwasg Gee, Denbigh, 1985.

    Bangor, Port of Beaumaris, Gwynedd Archives, 1988.

Williams, Rev. Peter Bayley, *The Tourist Guide Through the County of Caernarvon*, J. Hulme, Caernarfon, 1821.

Wynne, John, *Hanes Sir a Thre Caernarvon*, H. Humphreys, Caernarfon, 1861.